A LADY, KISS & TWO IDIOTS

Also, by S.K. Luke

Fictional

Milo the Cat – A Day Out

Villy the Vulture

Jeron and John – High and Fly

Ben the Bear

Who's in the Attic

Binny n Bonny

Bella's Boat Escapade

Tales of the Mochi Wala – The Cobbler

Silence Whispers

Unfaithful Desires

10.45 PM Show

Non-Fictional

Decoding Maturity

Navigating the Grey

I Lack Patience

You. Me. And The Space Between

A LADY, A KISS & TWO IDIOTS

S K Luke

Copyright

A Lady, A Kiss And Two Idiots

S.K. Luke

First Edition, 2025.

For permission requests or inquiries, please connect at:

SalimKhan27@gmail.com

.

ISBN: 978-93-5525-790-1

Contents

Behind The Madness

This book was born from too much imagination, quite a few plot twists, and just the right amount of chaos — fitting, considering the title. It began with a wild idea: a practical–romantic fusion featuring Melicia, the bold survivor of a man's world; Keith, the introverted gentleman who still believes in loyalty, sincerity, and quiet love; and Ryan — the chaos in Keith's life, the friend who brings headaches but stands firm when it truly matters.

Keith found love, but she wasn't what he expected. In fact, she was more than he could handle. Out of his league, unpredictable, dangerous in all the wrong and right ways — yet she liked him for exactly who he was. A simple man with a simple lifestyle, content with routine, honest intentions, and a quiet heart.

Melicia, a con artist who married wealthy men, took their money, and moved on to the next target, shattered Keith's peaceful life with cinematic mayhem — car chases, dangerous men, stolen heirlooms, schemes, cons, hiding, running, and every twist you'd expect in an action movie. Keith's world flipped the moment she walked into it. He and Ryan were swept into the madness, but Keith stood by her through every mess, and Ryan — being the loyal idiot he is — stood by Keith.

They might be idiots in the real world, but together, they survived. Together, they followed Melicia into danger and somehow crawled out alive, proving that even fools can be heroes with the right woman leading the way.

To my friends and family — your patience deserves a medal.

And to the readers: thank you for picking up A Lady, A Kiss, and Two Idiots. These characters are chaotic. They're flawed. They make terrible decisions. But they love fiercely — and so did I while shaping them into the versions you meet in this book.

This story exists because you're here, willing to go along for the ride

PREFACE

Melicia faked her death in a fiery car crash — not to escape love, but to escape the men hunting her. Van's men. They were closing in fast, and she made sure they believed she was gone. It was the only way to protect Keith, her husband, from the past she had buried too deeply.

But Keith never believed the lie.

For months, he searched quietly, obsessively — until Ryan, his best friend and full-time bad influence, stumbled across an Instagram photo.

Same smile. Same wrist scar. Same woman who once kissed Keith in the middle of a crowded street — sudden, reckless, unforgettable.

Keith followed the trail and, in classic Keith fashion, got himself nearly killed. Then Melicia appeared — saving his life like a ghost stepping out of memory. Overwhelmed, furious, and relieved all at once, he demanded the truth.

She told him everything.

Her past as a con artist.

The wealthy husbands she married and vanished from. Her marriage to Van — and how she stole a priceless family heirloom that sent his entire network hunting her across continents.

Keith still wanted her. And she, despite years of running, still loved him. But Melicia knew what Van did to the people she cared about — so she pushed Keith away, forcing herself to disappear from him all over again.

Keith returned to his old life — empty, restless, and increasingly drunk. Ryan, in his eternal wisdom, dragged him to a nightclub to "fix" things. Instead, they got tricked, scammed, and robbed.

Then Melicia called. She needed their help.

Or so she said.

It was a trap.

Keith walked straight into Van's hands, where he was thrown into a room with Melicia and Ryan. Van gave them forty-eight hours: return his heirloom, or die. The only problem? Melicia no longer had it. A pawn scammer had already sold it off.

Their hunt led them to Dr Stevens, a respected plastic surgeon, unknowingly in possession of the heirloom — until his fiancée, Diana Rods, stole it. And Diana wasn't working alone. She was Van's inside woman. The entire chase had been orchestrated.

Only Melicia saw the setup. She was already planning her counterstrike.

With help from her old partner-in-crime, Leo, she pulled off a masterful con: fake cops, a forged warrant, and a staged raid that framed Van for the theft of a famous painting, The Scarlet Veil. When his mansion was torn apart, the truth unravelled — the heirloom, the money, and Van's crimes lay bare.

Melicia had beaten him at his own game.

When everything finally settled, Melicia and Keith slipped into a quiet life. But quiet never suited her — the thrill had spoiled her too deeply.

So when trouble knocked again, she didn't run.

This time, she wasn't alone.

She had Keith — her husband, her weakness, and now… her partner in crime.

But that is a story for another time.

CHARACTERS

Arnold Melville – Banker

CSI Forensic Lead – Ashley Jolt

Diana Rods – Vans Stooge

Digger Miles – Star Pawn Owner

Dr Stevens – Plastic Surgeon

Florist – Woman in Prison

Henshaw – Keith's Office Boss

Joshua – Melicia's Cat

Kicth Miller – Librarian

Leo – Con Artist and Friend of Melica

Mary – Keith's Office Colleague

Melicia Miller – Keith's Wife and A Con Artist

Officer – Kirk Edmunds

Officer – Leann Phillips

Passerby – Shawn Binder

Ryan – Keith's Close Friend

Sunny – Bakery Boy

Thin Man –Thief

Travel Agency Manager – Jimmy Young

Turbo – Keith's Turtle Pet

Van Jeans – An Eccentric Wealthy Man

Woman in the Bar – Thief

Chapter 1

Flames On Highway 9

It was 4:50 AM, just before dawn.

The air was cool and damp, with mist hanging low over the road. The highway was quiet, except for the occasional hum of passing cars. Dew clung to the grass at the side of the road, glistening faintly in the dim light. The world felt still, with only the sound of tyres on the wet tarmac breaking the silence.

Then, out of nowhere, a speeding car shot past. Its headlights blazed, cutting through the mist like fiery eyes. As the car swerved into the fast lane, it overtook a slower vehicle so quickly that the driver barely noticed. The bright headlights flashed in the rear-view mirror, blinding the driver for a moment before the car sped away, its rear lights reflecting off the glass.

For a moment, the highway was flooded with bright light, blinding and sudden, before it disappeared, and the car vanished into the fog. The mist closed in, swallowing the headlights, and the highway was dark once more.

Then, there was a loud crash—the sound of metal twisting, followed by the shattering of glass. The speeding car collided violently with the side railing, smashing through it and hitting a lamp post. The force of the crash flipped the car and set it alight almost instantly.

Smoke quickly filled the air, swirling up into the sky, thick and black. The light from the burning wreck lit up the highway, flickering through the mist and casting eerie shadows on the road.

A car that had been following the speeding vehicle pulled over further down the highway. Its headlights were now the only light, as the streetlights had short-circuited from the crash. The man in the car got out quickly, his eyes widening at the sight of the burning wreckage.

The flames were fierce, and the heat radiated even from a distance. The lamp post that had been hit now hung dangerously, sparking as the electric wires caught fire. The whole scene seemed charged with danger, the air thick with smoke. The man didn't dare get any closer, not with the fire and the exposed wires crackling.

His hands shook as he took out his phone and dialled 999. "There's been an accident," he said, his voice tight. "A car's on fire, and the streetlights are out. You need to send help—now." He stayed back, watching the flames licking the sky, the crash still echoing in his mind. Everything felt frozen in that moment—the crash, the fire, the fear in the air.

As the man stared at the flames, one thought gnawed at him: Who was in that car? And, even more disturbing, how had it ended up like this?

He recorded a video of the burning car. As he did, he heard the siren of the highway patrol. The police officers got out of their vehicle, and the man paused his video as they approached.

“We got a distress call on the radio,” said one of the officers. “Are you the one who reported this?” He looked at the burning car. Meanwhile, the other officer was on the radio, rushing the fire brigade and ambulance to arrive as quickly as possible.

“I’m Shawn,” said the man, who had called the police, witnessed the crash, and filmed the incident.

Shawn stood back as the officers examined the scene, their expressions grim. The flames still flickered, casting long, dancing shadows across the wreckage. One of the officers, a woman with short brown hair, crouched beside the car, carefully inspecting the remains. She rose slowly, glancing back at Shawn.

“Did you see what happened? Was the driver going too fast?” she asked, her voice steady but edged with concern.

Shawn nodded, still staring at the fire. “Yes. The car was speeding. It overtook me just moments before the crash. I barely caught a glimpse of the driver… but I think it was a man.”

Another officer, tall and broad-shouldered with a thick beard, approached while speaking into his radio. “We need forensics down here immediately. It’s bad—awful.”

Shawn felt the weight of those words sink in. His hands were still trembling, and his mind whirled. Who was in that car? He thought again. The crash had been violent—too violent for anyone to have walked away.

One of the officers, noticing Shawn’s distracted look, stepped towards him. “Are you alright?” she asked gently. “We’ll need your details for a formal statement.”

“I’m alright,” Shawn replied quickly, though his voice was unsteady. “I just… I’ve never seen anything like this before. It all happened so quickly.”

The officer gave a brief nod and jotted down his details in her notebook. “Take a seat over there. Someone will speak with you shortly.”

Shawn drifted a little further from the wreck, his thoughts spinning. The flames had begun to die down, leaving only curling smoke and the blackened shell of what had once been a car.

A few minutes later, the same female officer returned with her colleague.

“I’m Officer Leann,” she said, offering a firm handshake. “And this is my partner, Officer Kirk. We’ll ask you more in a bit, but first we need to assess the scene.”

By now, the fire brigade had arrived. Their team moved swiftly and with practised precision, dousing the last of the flames with water. It was a careful operation, ensuring no remaining embers could reignite. Even from a distance, the heat was fierce. The car had been reduced to a twisted, blackened wreck. Steam hissed from the soaked metal as the final wisps of fire were extinguished.

Shawn watched from afar, his heart pounding. It was hard to believe someone had been inside that inferno just minutes earlier.

Once the fire was under control, Officers Leann and Kirk approached the vehicle. Leann crouched once more, scanning the twisted metal with a sharp eye.

“We need a closer look,” she said. She turned to Kirk and gestured. “Check the back. It’s leaning towards the slope. If the car hadn’t hit the barrier, it would’ve gone right down into the woods.”

Kirk nodded and cautiously made his way around the vehicle, his torch beam cutting through the lingering mist and smoke. The road was built along higher ground, and the slope beyond the barrier dropped steeply into dense woodland. It was a near miss.

He stopped by the rear door and peered inside, but the back seat was empty—no signs of life.

Meanwhile, Leann moved to the driver's side and examined the remains in the seat. The body was burnt beyond recognition. But the height, the build — it suggested a female.

"This is... grim," she muttered, standing slowly.

At the rear, Kirk used a crowbar to force open the boot. Inside was nothing but charred boxes and scorched bits of paper. The air still carried the harsh tang of burnt plastic and fuel. Smoke drifted lazily upwards from the metal frame.

"We need the forensic team urgently," Kirk said quietly. "This isn't good."

Leann nodded, then glanced over to the ambulance crew who had just arrived and were waiting nearby. She waved them off. "Hold back for now," she called. "There's nothing they can do at this point. We need to wait for forensics."

"Understood," replied one of the medics.

Leann stood up slowly, brushing her hands on her trousers as she looked around. The burnt-out car sat still, smoke rising faintly. The metal barrier was torn apart, and just beyond it, the slope dropped steeply into the woods. The area was quiet, apart from the occasional hiss from the wreck.

She turned to Kirk, her face serious.

"We need to know who was driving that car," she said firmly. "Looks like someone was speeding, maybe drunk. Some people don't value life."

Kirk nodded in agreement but noticed Shawn still standing a few steps away, looking dazed and disturbed. He walked over to him.

"You alright, mate?" Kirk asked gently.

Shawn looked up, startled. "Yeah… just can't get it out of my head. The whole thing happened right in front of me."

Kirk gave him a slight nod. "It's a lot to take in. If it's alright, we'll need your contact number. We may need to ask a few more questions later."

"Sure," said Shawn, pulling out his phone and reading out his number. Kirk jotted it down in his notebook.

"Thanks for your help tonight," Kirk said. "You did the right thing, calling it in."

Shawn gave a quiet nod, turned, and walked to his car. As he drove away, he glanced into the rear-view mirror one last time. The wreckage, flashing lights, and shadowy woods behind the scene stayed with him as he disappeared into the distance.

Back at the scene, the fire brigade had finished its work. The flames had been extinguished, and the car had cooled down. The ambulance crew waited nearby, while Officer Leann and Kirk kept the area secure.

Not long after, the forensic team arrived. A white van pulled up, and several experts stepped out, led by Ashley — a seasoned forensic officer with years of experience. He wore gloves and carried a small case of equipment.

"Evening," Ashley greeted as he approached Kirk and Leann. "We'll take over now. Can you give us a quick brief?"

Leann nodded. "Single car crash. The driver's body is still inside — badly burnt. No passengers. The car hit the railing, then the lamp post. Fire started on impact."

Ashley and his team quickly got to work. They cordoned off the area, placed evidence markers, and began taking photos from different angles. One team member carefully examined the crash site, while another began documenting the vehicle's interior.

Ashley came back a short while later, wiping his brow.

"From what I can see, this looks like a high-speed crash," he said. "The tyre skid marks show the driver tried to brake late. The car must've been doing at least 140 km/h before the impact."

"Any idea who the driver was?" Leann asked.

Ashley shook his head. "The body appears to be female. It could be young, but we can't say for certain. The burns are too severe. We've collected what we can — tissue and hair samples — for DNA testing. As for alcohol or drug use, we won't know until we get the post-mortem results."

"We'll move the body to the coroner's office," Ashley continued. "Should have something in the next day or so."

"This is going to be a long night," said Kirk, letting out a sigh.

The fire brigade, ambulance crew, and forensic team concluded their work and departed the scene. Ashley gave a final nod to the officers before heading off with the body.

Leann and Kirk stayed behind a bit longer to set up the police tape and secure the area. Once everything was in order, they returned to the station just before dawn. Their uniforms were dusty, their faces tired.

Inside the police station, just before their shift ended, Officers Leann and Kirk sat down with Station Chief Hardley.

Hardley leaned back in his chair, holding a mug of coffee. "Alright, what have we got?"

Kirk spoke up. "Looks like reckless driving, sir. Could've been speeding. Maybe alcohol was involved, but we're not sure yet."

Hardley raised an eyebrow. "Any idea who the victim is?"

Leann shook her head. "No ID on the body. Ashley's team is on it. They're running DNA tests and waiting for the post-mortem report."

"And the car?" asked Hardley.

Kirk checked his notes. "It's registered to a Regus travel agency. They open at nine — we'll give them a ring once they're in."

Hardley nodded slowly. "Good. Let's see what turns up. Keep me posted as soon as you get anything new."

"Yes, sir," they said together, then got up to leave.

Outside the Chief's office, Kirk rubbed his eyes and yawned. "That was one long night."

Leann chuckled weakly. "You're telling me."

They walked down to the car park. The early sun was already up, casting a soft orange glow over everything. The city was quiet, still half-asleep.

As they each headed to their cars, Leann glanced back at the station. "Reckless driving or not… something about this doesn't sit right."

Kirk nodded in agreement. "Feels like we're just scratching the surface."

They got into their cars and drove off, the weight of the case still hanging in the air.

Officer Leann was driving home, her thoughts still lingering on the wrecked car, the burnt body, and the strange feeling that something wasn't quite right. The night had felt like it would never end, and yet, she couldn't shake the feeling that there was more to this case than a simple accident.

Without even realising, she had taken a wrong turn — or maybe it wasn't a mistake at all.

Leann made a sharp U-turn, heading back towards the accident site. The early morning sun cast a hazy glow over the road, but the scene still felt grim, the echoes of the crash still hanging in the air. She parked her car by the side of the road and stepped out slowly. The remnants of the burnt car had long since been towed away, but the smell of scorched rubber and charred metal still lingered.

The road, a winding hilltop stretch, seemed peaceful now. But looking at the curve ahead, Leann couldn't understand why the driver had been speeding so recklessly. It was a sharp curve — an accident waiting to happen.

She crouched down, studying the tyre marks still visible on the road. The skid marks were long, a clear sign that the driver had tried to brake, but it had been too late. The car had been travelling at high speed — far too fast for a curve like this.

Leann picked up her phone, swiping the screen to call Ashley.

"Ashley, it's me, Leann," she said when he answered. "Do you have anything for me on the victim yet?"

Ashley's voice was calm, but Leann could hear the tiredness in it. "Not yet, I'm still waiting on some lab results. I'll share the details as soon as I have them."

Leann sighed, looking out at the road. "And what about the car? The tyre marks... Do you suggest anything unusual, any foul play?"

There was a pause before Ashley spoke again. "Based on the initial findings, it looks like an accident. No signs of foul play so far. But we can't conclude anything until we know more about the victim."

Leann looked back at the winding road one last time. The area was calm, but the feeling in her gut hadn't gone away. "Understood," she said softly, ending the call.

She stood there for a moment, taking it all in. The road had an eerie quiet about it now, a stark contrast to the chaos that had unfolded here hours earlier. Leann couldn't shake the nagging feeling that something had been missed. The sharp curve in the road had been a dangerous spot, but why had the driver been going so fast? It seemed too predictable, too easy for the accident to happen this way.

She lifted her gaze, scanning the surroundings for anything that might offer a clue. Her eyes swept the area, but there was nothing — no CCTV cameras, no hidden surveillance. This stretch of road was clear of such technology. She exhaled slowly, the lack of evidence only adding to the weight of her thoughts.

Nearby, workers from the municipal corporation were busy reinstalling the electric lamp post that had been struck in the crash. The hum of their machinery filled the silence as they worked to restore the streetlights that had been knocked out by the accident.

The quiet buzz of activity was in stark contrast to the heavy feeling that pressed against Leann's chest.

The accident had been written to happen, she thought. But why? The speed, the skidding tyres — everything had aligned too perfectly, too easily.

Leann turned, her shoes crunching on the gravel as she headed back to her car. She couldn't shake the unease that had settled deeper within her. This wasn't just a random accident, and she knew it. Some questions need answers.

Sliding into her car, she stared at the road one last time before starting the engine. Her mind was racing. She had to focus and get some rest.

The town was quiet, as it always was. Not much ever happened here. It was a peaceful, slow-paced place — far removed from the bustling city. But now, with this case, everything felt different. Leann knew she couldn't let this go. It was too important, and something was lurking in the shadows that she needed to uncover.

With a sigh, she drove home, the quiet of the countryside filling the space around her, but her thoughts were anything but still.

Leann was deeply asleep, her body craving rest after the long night shift. The quiet of her room was a welcome change, but it didn't last long. Her phone rang, cutting through the peaceful silence.

She groggily reached for it, her eyes half-open. The name on the screen was familiar. Ashley.

"Leann… It's Ashley," came his voice, sharp but tinged with professionalism. "We've identified the victim. Her name's Melicia Horton. She lives at 56 Sterling Street. No sign of alcohol, no foul play. Looks like a clean accident, but we're still digging into her background."

Leann's mind struggled to keep up. She wiped sleep from her eyes, forcing herself to focus. "Melicia Horton… married?"

"Her husband's Keith Horton," Ashley continued. "We'll dig deeper, but that's all we've got so far."

Leann nodded, even though Ashley couldn't see her. "Thanks, Ashley. Keep me posted."

She hung up and stared at the ceiling, the exhaustion still weighing heavily on her, but the case gnawing at her thoughts. She quickly grabbed her phone again and called Officer Kirk.

The phone rang twice before Kirk answered, his voice thick with sleep. "Leann? What's up?"

"Get up, Kirk," she said, though her voice was softer than usual, still half-asleep. "I need you to dig into this, Melicia Horton and her husband, Keith. Find out everything. I don't care if it's personal stuff. We need to know what we're dealing with here."

Kirk groaned. "I'll get on it, but I need sleep, Leann. You know how long these cases take… especially now that it's picked up steam."

"Just get me the details, Kirk."

"Yeah, yeah…" Kirk sighed, rubbing his eyes. He sat up in bed for a moment, still groggy. His mind flickered to the long shift ahead — one that was only going to get longer with this case. "Alright, I'm on it. I'll put the others on it too so that we can cover more ground."

"Ok," Leann replied. "And Kirk... get some rest. We'll need you sharp for later."

"Sure, sure…" Kirk mumbled as he hung up. As soon as the call ended, he let out a tired sigh, the weight of his exhaustion settling back on him. He called in the other officers at the station, briefed them on the situation, and asked them to quickly gather as much information as possible on the victim, Melicia Horton, and her husband, Keith.

With the details shared and tasks delegated, Kirk collapsed back into bed, pulling the covers up over him. He knew sleep wouldn't come easily, but he needed it. The case would demand more from him soon, and he knew it wouldn't be a quiet shift when he returned.

A couple of hours later, Kirk's phone buzzed on the nightstand, its vibration loud enough to pierce the silence. He groaned, rolled over, and squinted at the screen. A message from the station—it was the report.

Still half-asleep, he rubbed his eyes and forwarded the info to Officer Leann. Then, dragging himself out of bed, he shuffled into the kitchen—hair tousled, shirt wrinkled. He brewed himself a strong black coffee, sat down, and sipped slowly, letting the warmth bring him back to life.

Another buzz.

Leann: "Got the info. Are we heading to talk to the husband?"

Kirk took another sip, then tapped back a quick reply.

Kirk: "I'll come pick you up."

He downed the rest of his coffee, took a quick shower, changed into clean clothes, and grabbed his keys. Outside, the sun hung low in the sky—bright, but doing little to ease his fatigue. He cracked the window as he drove, hoping the breeze would help him stay sharp.

When he pulled up outside Leann's building, she was already waiting on the curb. She slid into the passenger seat, ponytail tight, eyes sharp.

"It's 5 p.m.," she said with a small smile. "Guess a 'good evening' is in order."

"Barely good," Kirk muttered, starting the engine. "Feels like it's going to be one of those shifts."

They drove in silence for a moment, the city rolling past in a blur of fading light and traffic noise. Then Leann glanced over.

"Have you talked to the rental agency yet? The one the car's registered to?"

Kirk shook his head. "Not yet. Once we got Melicia's details, I figured we'd get more out of going straight to the source. Face-to-face tends to shake more truth loose."

Leann frowned slightly, arms crossed. "Maybe. But a quick call could've given us a lead on where she was headed. Could've changed how we handle Keith."

He nodded. "You're right. I'll follow up with them after we talk to him."

Leann exhaled through her nose. "Let's just hope Keith gives us something solid."

Kirk smirked. "If he doesn't… You know we'll dig."

They drove on, the silence comfortable now, both officers switching into work mode as the car rolled toward 56 Sterling Street.

As they pulled into the driveway of the modest two-storey house at 56 Sterling Street, Kirk parked at the kerb and switched off the engine. The house appeared quiet—blinds half-drawn, a blue Sudan car parked neatly in the driveway.

Kirk glanced at Leann. "You ready?"

Leann gave a short nod. "Always. Are you taking the lead, or shall I?"

Kirk raised an eyebrow. "You take the lead on this one—I need to refocus."

She smirked. "Still waking up?"

Kirk chuckled as he unbuckled his seatbelt. "Let's both handle it. You read his body language; I'll push if we need to."

They walked up to the front door and rang the bell. After a few moments, the door opened slowly. Keith stood there—dishevelled, anxious.

"Did you find anything about my missing wife?" he asked, voice strained.

"I'm Officer Kirk, and this is Officer Leann," Kirk said, holding up his badge. "We're here about your wife, Melicia."

"Please, come in," Keith said, stepping aside.

Inside, the living room was spotless—too spotless. Cushions were perfectly aligned, the surfaces gleamed, and a faint aroma of stale coffee lingered in the air, as though it had been brewed hours ago but never touched.

They sat opposite Keith, who perched on the edge of the sofa like a guest in his own home.

Leann broke the silence. "We received the report. Some things aren't quite adding up."

Keith looked up, eyes wide. "Like what?"

Kirk leaned forward slightly. "For starters, what was your wife doing in a hired car? We noticed your vehicle, the blue Sudan, parked right outside."

Keith blinked. "I—I wasn't aware she'd hired a car. Have you found her? Please, I want to know where she is." His voice cracked. "We had a row two nights ago. I went out for dinner, came back, and had words. Nothing serious. She was upset, so she slept in the adjoining room. I didn't disturb her—I just went to bed in the spare room."

Kirk and Leann sat quietly, overseeing him.

"In the morning, she was gone," Keith continued. "Her phone was switched off. I tried everything—called her friends, the hotel where she works. No one had seen or heard from her."

Leann got up and slowly paced the room, eyes scanning the surroundings. The walls were lined with photos of Keith and Melicia—holidays, birthdays, candid smiles. A couple that, at least on the surface, seemed happy.

“Go on, Mr Horton,” Kirk prompted.

“I reported her missing last night,” Keith added quietly. “At the local station. Isn’t that why you’re here?”

Leann turned to face him, frowning slightly. “You reported her missing last night?”

“Yes.”

She glanced at Kirk, and they exchanged a look. Something didn’t sit right.

Kirk exhaled. “Mr Horton, I’m sorry to be the one to tell you this, but your wife was involved in a car accident. The vehicle caught fire. The victim inside—believed to be Melicia—was found in a burnt-out hire car, about 45 miles from here.”

Keith stared at him, stunned. “No. No, it can’t be her. Why would she even be in a hired car? You must have the wrong person.”

“We need you to come with us to identify the body,” Leann said gently.

Keith stood abruptly. “Let’s go. I want to see for myself.”

Without another word, he closed the door, turned the key in the lock, and followed them out. Kirk and Leann climbed into the police car, while Keith slipped into his vehicle and fell in behind them.

As they drove, Kirk cast her a sidelong glance. “You could’ve asked him to come down to the station—or even the hospital. Why turn up at his house like that?”

Leann kept her eyes fixed on the road, her tone calm but deliberate. “I wanted to see his reaction. Something about this accident doesn’t sit right with me. I needed to look him in the eye when we told him.”

“And now?” Kirk asked quietly. “What did you see?”

She hesitated. “He looked genuinely shaken. But it’s hard to be certain. His timeline needs checking—especially that business about filing a report last night.”

Kirk muttered, annoyance creeping into his voice. “I rang the station. Keith had already put in a missing person’s report. How on earth did they not tell us, knowing full well we’re running this case?”

Leann gave a wry smile. “Same old story. Lads at the station can’t be trusted to do their jobs properly. No surprise there.”

Kirk nodded grimly. “According to Ashley’s report, Keith’s a librarian. Teaches German part-time. Melicia works at the local bank. On the surface, they’re as ordinary as they come.”

“That’s just it,” Leann murmured. “They’re a bit too ordinary.

“Kirk gave her a sideways glance. “You think there’s more to this than a domestic row gone bad?”

She shrugged slightly. “Something’s off. I don’t know what yet, but my gut says this isn’t as clean as it looks.”

They drove on in silence, each officer deep in thought as the road stretched ahead of them.

Chapter 2

Nothing But A Tattoo

The hospital was quiet at this hour, its corridors dimly lit and hushed, with only the occasional squeak of trolley wheels or distant beep of machines.

Kirk and Officer Leann walked beside Keith, who had barely said a word since getting into the car. His steps were slow, hesitant. The weight of uncertainty clung to him like a second skin.

The coroner met them, a greying man in a sterile white coat. He gave them a solemn nod. “This way, please.”

He led them down a narrow corridor, growing colder and quieter with each step. The hum of fluorescent lights buzzed overhead. Keith’s breathing grew shallow.

They entered the morgue—sterile, still, and dreadfully cold.

The coroner walked to a covered gurney and paused. “Are you ready?” he asked gently.

Keith nodded, though it was barely perceptible.

The sheet was pulled back slowly.

Beneath it lay a body, burnt beyond recognition—charred skin, stiff limbs. The features were unidentifiable.

Keith took a step back, his face contorting in pain.

"Is... is that her?" he choked.

Kirk looked at the coroner, who answered in a flat tone, "DNA results confirmed it's Melicia."

Keith's knees buckled slightly. His voice cracked. "I... I don't believe it. It can't be her." His eyes brimmed with tears. "This—this isn't possible."

Officer Leann, calm but observant, asked, "Is there anything on the body you can recognise? Something distinct—tattoos, scars, anything unusual?"

Keith swallowed hard. He took a hesitant step forward and peered closer. Then, his eyes widened slightly.

"There—on her left shoulder... the tattoo. We got it when we were in Bali. Just a few months ago."

He pointed to the faint remains of ink amidst the burns.

"That's her. That's Melicia."

The room fell silent.

Kirk looked at Leann. She didn't say a word, but her brows had drawn together slightly—something felt off.

She turned to the coroner. "Were any personal items found? Jewellery, handbag, phone?"

The coroner shook his head. "Nothing. No belongings, no wedding ring, no purse. Not even an ID."

Kirk frowned. "That's unusual."

"Possibly thrown from the car in the crash," the coroner offered. "Or burnt. The fire was intense."

"There's no sign of foul play?" Leann asked.

"None. According to the eyewitness—Shawn Binder—a car sped past him recklessly and crashed into a post. He reported the fire moments later. No other vehicles were involved. It all points to an accident."

Keith suddenly turned and briskly walked out of the morgue.

Kirk and Leann followed him.

"We'll need a day or so to wrap this up," Leann called after him. "We'll be in touch."

But Keith didn't respond. He reached his car, got in, and drove off.

Kirk watched him disappear down the road. "He's broken," he muttered.

Leann crossed her arms; her eyes still fixed in the direction Keith had gone.

"Something about this doesn't sit right with me."

Kirk nodded slowly. "No personal items. Burnt beyond recognition. A husband confirming identity through a tattoo."

"He knew exactly where to look," she added. "Too quickly."

Kirk exhaled heavily, his gaze drifting back to the hospital doors.

"Right," he said at last. "Let's head to the travel agency. See where she was going… if she ever meant to leave at all."

At the agency, Jimmy, the manager, was already waiting for them. Spotting the officers, he stepped forward and held the door wide.

"Good evening, officers," he greeted, a little too brightly. "I've got everything you asked for."

He led them to a counter at the back, where a small monitor was set up. With a click, grainy footage began to play. There she was—Melicia—walking in, speaking to the receptionist, producing her licence, paying by card. Her face was unmistakable.

Kirk leaned on the counter, eyes narrowing. "All looks perfectly ordinary to me."

Jimmy nodded firmly. "We followed the procedure. I checked her licence, verified her identity, and collected payment in full. Everything was legitimate—no reason to doubt it."

"There—her left shoulder. The tattoo," Officer Kirk pointed out.

Leann crossed her arms, frowning. "That settles it, then. Melicia herself rented the car… which puts her behind the wheel when it crashed." She turned to Jimmy. "We'll need a copy of this recording."

"Absolutely," Jimmy said quickly, sliding a drive into the port.

Back in their car, heading towards the station, the silence lingered for a moment before Leann spoke.

"It does look like an accident. No sign of foul play. What I can't work out is why she hired a car at all, when they've already got one at home."

Kirk shrugged, keeping his eyes on the road. "Maybe she didn't want to use Keith's. Maybe she wanted distance—from him, from her life. Somewhere, she thought she couldn't be found. If she were driving recklessly, it could explain the crash."

Leann shook her head slowly. "Perhaps. But I'm not convinced. Something about Keith still doesn't sit right with me. I've no evidence—yet—but the pieces don't quite fit."

Back at home, Keith sat slumped on the sofa, the silence of the house pressing in on him. His eyes fixed on the framed photograph of Melicia perched atop the bookshelf beside the television. He whispered under his breath, almost as if the glass itself might answer him.

"You knew this day would come, didn't you, Keith? She was never truly yours… not in the way you thought."

The thought gnawed at him. He had sensed it long before, back in Bali just months ago. That holiday should have been bliss, a chance to rekindle what little spark they had left. Instead, it had shown him something he hadn't wanted to admit.

He closed his eyes, the memory rising unbidden. They had been walking through the crowded streets, the scent of incense and sea air heavy in the air, when Melicia tugged at his hand and pointed.

"Darling, look—a tattoo parlour. I'd love one. I've always wanted one."

Keith frowned. "It's nothing but torture, all that pain for something you'll regret in a few years."

She folded her arms, smirking. "Hmph. You could at least pretend to support me." Her tone dripped with sarcasm.

Before he could argue further, she had pulled him through the door. Inside, the walls were lined with designs, and a woman at the counter called for an artist, who stepped out— a tall, well-built man with dark hair and an easy smile.

"I'm Rock," he said, his eyes flicking briefly to Melicia. "So, who's after a tattoo?"

Keith noticed the way Rock's gaze lingered just a little too long on her, and worse, the way Melicia's lips curved into a playful smile in return. A silent current passed between them—one Keith felt immediately, like a sting.

"It's for my wife," Keith cut in, forcing the words out as he stepped slightly closer to her, breaking their eye contact.

"Oh, sure," Rock said casually, beckoning Melicia to sit.

She chose a design quickly and settled into the chair, lifting her dress just enough to expose the curve of her hip. Keith watched, his jaw tight, as the artist leaned in, the air thick with their teasing exchanges. From time to time, Melicia glanced at Keith with a mischievous look, as if daring him to react.

When it was over, she admired the fresh ink, thanked Rock far too sweetly, and walked out into the night air with Keith trailing silently beside her.

"Darling, you're quiet," she said after a while, her tone half-mocking, half-curious. "Did it bother you?"

Keith forced a thin smile. "Not at all. I was just surprised to see… this side of you."

Melicia laughed, brushing her hair back. "Oh, come now. I was only teasing. He was attractive, I'll admit, but not my type." She leaned closer, her eyes sparkling. "You are my type, my love. The most caring, loving man I've ever known. I only wanted to see your reaction." She giggled and kissed his cheek, leaving him unsure whether to believe her.

Keith snapped back to the present, his chest heavy. The memory soured as he muttered bitterly into the silence of the room.

"You never made sense, Melicia. Never. Always playing games."

His hands clenched into fists. The picture frame stared back at him, her smile frozen, mocking. He shook his head sharply.

"It wasn't you in that morgue. I know it wasn't. Your tattoo was on your hip, not your shoulder. They're blind, all of them—Kirk, Leann, the whole lot. Blind."

He pressed his palms into his eyes, forcing back the rising frustration.

"I could tell them. I should tell them. But no… no, not yet. Better to wait, better to see what you're up to." His voice broke into a whisper. "What are you planning, Melicia? Why vanish like this? Why leave me with nothing but questions?"

The weight of the silence closed in on him again, and Keith sat rigid in the dim light of the living room, caught between grief, suspicion, and the chilling certainty that his wife was out there somewhere—watching, waiting, playing a game only she knew the rules to.

At the station, Kirk set about drafting the case summary. His report was concise, factual, and by-the-book. Once his superior's signature was on it, the body was formally released.

The following day, the funeral was arranged with disquieting haste, as though the matter needed to be done and dusted before anyone asked too many questions. Keith carried himself with a measured calm, his shoulders squared, his steps steady. To the casual observer, he appeared to be a grieving widower keeping his composure. Inside, however, the truth pressed on him like a lead weight.

It isn't her, he thought, his eyes fixed on the coffin. That poor woman they pulled from the wreckage… she wasn't Melicia. And yet here I am, burying her as if she were.

The danger of it all prickled at the back of his neck. If he revealed his suspicions, if he dared to say aloud that the body wasn't his wife, suspicion could turn swiftly upon him. The last thing he wanted was to be accused of murdering the very person he believed was still alive, somewhere out there. For now, silence was survival.

The service itself was subdued—eerily so. A thin scattering of neighbours filled the pews, their whispered condolences sounding rehearsed, almost perfunctory. Their words carried politeness, not grief. Keith endured their handshakes and clumsy platitudes with rigid formality, his face unreadable, his voice flat. A few of Melicia's former colleagues drifted in as well, their expressions tight with polite obligation rather than genuine sorrow. No tears were shed for her; no true lament was heard.

From the back of the chapel, Kirk and Leann observed quietly. Both still wore plain clothes, their faces drawn from a sleepless night shift. They said nothing, but their eyes missed little. The room's emptiness spoke for itself. Either Melicia had lived a fiercely private life, or she had left behind few real ties.

When the final hymn faltered and faded, the handful of mourners began to disperse. Keith, however, remained rooted at the front, his gaze fixed on the coffin. His eyes were dry, his face a mask that revealed nothing. He lingered longer than anyone else, as if measuring the moment, as if weighing what came next.

At the rear, Kirk exhaled softly, leaning just enough for his words to reach Leann.

"End of the line for her."

Leann's gaze flicked sideways, her jaw tightening, her voice pitched low.

"Or the beginning of something we've yet to understand."

The coffin began its slow descent, the sound of the mechanism echoing hollowly through the near-empty chapel. Keith did not flinch. His lips moved ever so slightly, a whisper meant for no one's ears but his own.

You're out there, Melicia. I know you are. And whatever this is… I'll play along, for now.

Chapter 3

And Then It Came

A few days later, Keith found himself back at the library, the hushed corridors and the familiar scent of ageing books providing an oddly comforting solace. The quiet, meticulous rhythm of his work offered a thin veil of normality, keeping his mind engaged while he tucked away the restless unease that lingered just beneath the surface.

"Keith," called his colleague, Mary, from behind the reference desk, "it's good to see you back. I know it's been... difficult." She offered a sympathetic smile.

Keith gave a faint nod, absently organising a stack of new arrivals. "Yes, well... it's time to get on with things, isn't it?" His tone was even, almost rehearsed.

Mary leaned closer. "If you need someone to talk to... or even just a break, don't hesitate."

"I appreciate it," Keith replied softly, avoiding her gaze. "I just... want to keep busy."

Even his boss, Mr Henshaw, noticed. "Keith, if you need more time off, don't hesitate. It's perfectly understandable."

"No, thank you," Keith said firmly, straightening his posture. "Back to work. Keeps the mind off things."

The evenings offered little relief. His part-time German lessons served as both a financial necessity and a welcome distraction. Occasionally, his students would ask politely, "Alles in Ordnung, Herr Keith? Sie wirken verloren." He'd respond with a faint smile and carry on with his routine — the only thing that still gave him a sense of control.

At work, Keith was little more than a shadow of the man he used to be — withdrawn, muted, and moving through the days as though on borrowed time. At home, the nights blended into one another, the pale flicker of the television casting restless patterns across the walls. A half-finished glass of whisky sat beside him, untouched for hours, as he sat in deliberate isolation — apart from friends, neighbours, and anyone who might disturb the fragile silence he had built around himself.

The phone rang often. Messages stacked up, calls from concerned acquaintances scrolling unanswered on the screen. Sometimes, there was a knock at the door—persistent, almost pleading. Keith ignored them all. Even when Ryan's voice carried through the wood— "Open the door, I know you're in there!"—Keith remained still, unmoving. The company was no comfort. Solitude was the only refuge he trusted.

Only Turbo, his turtle, was permitted into that private world. Keith fed her, watched her wander in her unhurried way, sometimes speaking softly as though she could understand. She became his one confidante—quiet, constant—when everything else felt uncertain, broken.

He missed Melicia with a weight that hollowed him out. She had always seemed a little out of reach, too radiant, too extraordinary. And yet, once, she had chosen him. He held fast to that, convincing himself there must have been a reason she left, that if ever she needed him again, he would be ready, waiting.

But in the stillness, the doubt always returned, insistent and cold: Do not trust your heart. The marriage was faltering. It was always going to end this way.

Unbeknownst to him, Officer Leann had kept an eye from afar. She noted his routines and solitary habits, watching with a quiet suspicion. Something about Keith never quite settled with her. Yet as months slipped by—six in total—the man's life remained unchanged. He worked, he taught, he returned home to his quiet house, and nothing overtly suspicious occurred.

Leann sighed one evening, leaning back in her chair at the station. "Perhaps… perhaps it is over," she muttered. She had double-checked: Keith had not filed any insurance claims, made any sudden withdrawals, or shown any signs of financial motive. All things considered, it seemed genuine. If Melicia had vanished… perhaps she had not survived after all.

With a reluctant shake of her head, Leann allowed herself to return to her regular duties. Her instincts still whispered that something didn't add up—but for now, she would set the matter aside.

Meanwhile, in his quiet house, Keith poured another drink and stared into the amber liquid, muttering under his breath:

"Six months… and still, no answers."

He glanced at the clock. Evening had descended into silence. He would sit alone, as he had every night, as he intended to do for the foreseeable future. No phone calls, no visitors, no distractions—just himself, his thoughts, and the carefully constructed solitude he had built.

He was hoping she would walk in from that front door and return to him.

That Friday evening, Keith trudged up the narrow stairwell, his backpack slung low, every step heavy with the dull rhythm of routine. He slid his key into the lock—then froze.

"Keith!" a voice rang out.

He turned. Ryan was leaning against the banister, grinning like he owned the place.

"What the hell are you doing here?" Keith asked flatly.

"It's Friday, mate." Ryan pushed his hair out of his face, still grinning. "You should be out at a pub, pint in hand, not rotting away in some dusty library. I came to rescue you from your hermit life."

Keith shoved the door open, not bothering to hide his irritation. "Not interested. Not tonight."

Ryan slipped in right behind him, ignoring the dismissal, shutting the door with a soft click. "Fine, fine. But I've got something you need to see."

Keith dumped his bag on the floor with a thud. "What now?"

Ryan pulled out his phone and held it up like a trophy. "This. Just watch. Humour me for five seconds."

Keith waved him off. "I don't—"

"Keith," Ryan pressed, thrusting the phone closer, "just look. The woman in this video… tell me she doesn't look familiar."

With a sharp sigh, Keith snatched the phone. On-screen, a shaky Instagram reel played—someone filming their coffee in a bustling street. But in the corner, half-obscured and striding past in dark sunglasses—

Keith's breath caught. His pulse spiked. "Melicia…" he whispered.

Ryan shifted uneasily. "I thought the same. Could be a twin, right? A lookalike?"

Keith replayed the clip, freezing it, leaning closer until his nose almost touched the screen. "Glasgow," he murmured, reading the geotag. His hands tightened on the phone. "This was posted yesterday?"

"Yeah. Yesterday." Ryan's voice had lost its playful edge. "I tried calling you. You didn't pick up."

Keith ignored him, eyes locked on the frozen frame. "It's her. Sunglasses or not… It's her walk. Her posture. She's alive."

Ryan's mouth went dry. "Keith, we buried her. We saw the body."

Keith turned, his eyes blazing. "We buried someone. But it wasn't Melicia."

Ryan's face drained of colour. "You're serious. You actually believe this."

"I don't believe," Keith snapped, tossing the phone back at him. "I know." He moved swiftly, yanking open drawers, stuffing clothes into a bag.

Ryan ran a hand down his face. "Mate… you've lost it. This is an obsession, not proof."

Keith zipped the bag, his movements sharp and final. "Call it what you want. I'm going to Glasgow."

Ryan stared at him, torn between disbelief and fear. "And if it's not her?"

Keith's jaw tightened. "Then I'll know for sure. But if it is…" He slung the bag over his shoulder. "Then everything changes."

He brushed past Ryan, heading for the door.

Ryan called after him, his voice cracking with something between anger and worry. “Keith! For God’s sake—what if you’re chasing a ghost?”

Keith didn’t turn back. He opened the door and stepped into the night, leaving Ryan standing in the middle of the flat, clutching his phone, the video still looping endlessly in his hand.

Ryan sighed, knowing there was no reasoning with him. “Mate… think about this.”

Keith shot him a glance, cold and resolute. “I have. There’s no thinking about it anymore. She’s out there, and I’m going to find her.”

Ryan pulled his car out of the driveway. Keith tossed his travel bag into the back seat and slid in beside him. The drive to the airport unfolded in silence — Ryan stealing uneasy glances at his friend, while Keith stared straight ahead, lost somewhere deep in thought.

Suddenly, Keith turned. “Turbo — my turtle.” He rummaged for his keys and pressed them into Ryan’s hand. “Here, my house keys. Feed Turbo daily — his food’s on the dining table.”

Ryan gave a quick nod.

“Don’t just nod,” Keith said sharply. “Make sure you take care of him. And no girls in my house.”

Ryan nodded again, keeping his eyes on the road. He knew Keith was wound tight and decided not to push it.

When they finally reached the terminal, Keith was out of the car before it had even rolled to a stop.

“Keith! Wait!” Ryan called after him, but Keith was already gone — weaving through the crowd of passengers, eyes fixed on the departure board, his pace quickening with every step.

Ryan stood at the curb, watching his friend disappear into the crowd, his chest tight with dread. Under his breath, he whispered, "God help you, Keith… whatever you think you're chasing."

Inside, Keith pushed through security, his heart thudding in his chest, every nerve taut and wired to a single purpose: finding her—unravelling the truth that had gnawed at him for six long months.

He'd managed to secure a last-minute ticket to Glasgow. It was a late-night flight, which meant hours to kill in the sterile glow of the airport. With his bag slung at his side, he found an empty bench near Gate 27 and dropped into it, his luggage pulled close against his leg.

He took out his phone, thumbs hovering before he typed: Please feed Turbo. In this rush, I forgot all about her.

A few minutes later, Ryan replied: "Will do. Don't worry, mate. If you need me, let me know—I'll be there for you, buddy."

Keith stared at the glowing screen, the corners of his mouth twitching into the faintest smile. At least someone's got my back, he thought, feeling a small flicker of warmth cut through the dullness that had settled over him. He slipped the phone back into his pocket and leaned against the cold metal bench, exhaling slowly.

Time crawled. The airport around him was alive in a rhythm of its own—families corralling sleepy children in matching hoodies, business travellers hunched over their laptops, faces lit by the ghostly blue of spreadsheets, and couples lost in each other's quiet laughter, hands intertwined as if the world outside the terminal no longer existed.

Overhead, the Tannoy system crackled to life again and again, the same flat voice echoing through the hall: flight numbers, destinations, gate changes — an endless loop of noise that mingled with the soft clatter of coffee cups and the hum of rolling luggage.

Keith's eyes drifted to the large windows overlooking the tarmac. Planes taxied in and out, their lights blinking like restless stars in the foggy night. He checked his watch, then his phone, then his watch again — time refusing to move.

Boredom settled over him like a fog. He leaned back, folding his arms. Just for a moment, he told himself, letting his eyelids fall. The hum of the airport faded into a gentle blur — footsteps, muffled voices, the distant whir of jet engines — all blending into a dull, soothing rhythm.

When the shake came, it jolted him upright. A hand gripped his shoulder — firm but not harsh.

"Sir? Are you Keith?"

Keith blinked, his mind scrambling to catch up. A uniformed security guard stood over him, the man's radio crackling faintly at his belt.

"Yes… Yes, that's me," Keith muttered, rubbing his eyes.

"Your flight to Glasgow is making its final boarding call," the guard said. "They've been calling your name over the PA. If you don't go now, you'll miss it."

Keith shot up, heart pounding as adrenaline surged through the fatigue. "Goodness—yes. Right. Thanks!"

He grabbed his bag, nearly stumbling as he broke into a half-run down the terminal. His trainers slapped against the polished floor, weaving past bewildered travellers. He could hear the gate staff's voices echoing:

"Final call for passenger Keith Miller, flight 739 to Glasgow."

"Wait! I'm here!" Keith shouted, breathless, waving his boarding pass like a lifeline.

The gate attendant gave him a look equal parts irritation and relief. "Cutting it a bit fine, aren't we, Mr Miller?"

"You've no idea," Keith muttered, forcing a weary grin.

He hurried down the jet bridge, lungs burning, and dropped into his seat just as the cabin doors sealed shut behind him. He exhaled hard, his heart still hammering. Nearly missed it, he thought. And after all this… I can't afford mistakes.

An hour and a half later, the flight touched down in Glasgow just as dawn broke, the sky a muted grey smudged with streaks of pale gold. Keith's body ached with fatigue, his head foggy from a night without rest. But his nerves still buzzed too much for sleep. He slung his bag over his shoulder and staggered through the arrivals hall, blinking against the sterile light.

Glasgow waited. And somewhere within it—Melicia.

Outside, the cold air bit at his cheeks. He hailed the first cab he saw and slid into the back seat, fumbling his phone from his pocket. Pulling up the blurred Instagram still, he leaned forward and showed it to the driver.

"Can you take me here?" Keith asked, his voice hoarse.

The cabbie squinted at the picture, then gave a knowing grunt. "Aye, that's Buchanan Street. Busy spot. I'll get you there."

Keith nodded, sinking into the seat as the cab rattled away from the airport. His eyes burned with exhaustion, but every corner they turned tightened the knot in his chest. When they finally stopped, he paid the driver without counting the change and stepped out onto the pavement.

The street buzzed with early morning life—commuters with coffees, shopkeepers pulling up shutters, the distant clang of a busker setting up. Keith stood frozen for a moment, scanning the faces, hoping.

Nothing. Just strangers in their world.

His stomach growled. Across the road, a small bakery with steamed-up windows beckoned. He pushed through the door, the warmth and smell of fresh bread enveloping him. A bell tinkled overhead.

"One tea," Keith muttered to the young man behind the counter. "And… whatever's fresh."

"Got doughnuts just out of the fryer," the boy replied cheerfully.

Keith nodded, paid, and slumped at a table near the window. He stared out at the street as he sipped the hot tea, letting the warmth ease his throat. Every passer-by, every silhouette made his heart jolt for a moment—until the truth hit: not her.

He wolfed down the doughnuts, wiped his hands on a napkin, and stood again. Determined.

For the next hour, Keith scoured the street, walking into jewellers, designer boutiques, perfume shops—anywhere Melicia would have drifted, given her taste for expensive, lavish things. "Excuse me, have you seen this woman?" he repeatedly asked, showing the grainy photo on his phone. Most shook their heads. Some barely looked before dismissing him. A few gave polite smiles, then turned away.

Hope frayed with each rejection.

By noon, Keith found himself back at the bakery, drained and with a dry throat. He ordered another tea and a pastry, but barely tasted them.

The boy from behind the counter approached his table, curiosity in his eyes. "You've been here since morning. Wandering up and down, showing folk that picture. Are you looking for someone?"

Keith's hands trembled as he turned his phone around, showing the blurred shot of Melicia in sunglasses. "Her. Have you seen her?"

The boy frowned, studying it carefully. Then his eyes lit up. "Yeah... aye, I think I have. A couple of days ago. Came in here. She ordered a coffee and a croissant, but—" he hesitated, glancing at Keith, "—she left in a hurry. Didn't even wait for it."

Keith's chest tightened. "Are you sure?"

The boy nodded. "I remember cause it was odd. She kept looking over her shoulder, like she didn't want to be seen."

Keith sat back, his pulse hammering. She had been here. Not months ago. Days. Close enough that he could almost feel her shadow lingering.

"Thank you," Keith whispered. His tea sat untouched now, hands clenched in fists on the table. His exhaustion was gone—burned away by a single thought. She was alive. And she was running from something.

The bakery bell jingled as a pair of customers stepped inside, their voices mixing with the smell of fresh bread and butter rolls. Outside, the street was alive with honking cars, bicycles weaving between traffic, and pedestrians clutching shopping bags. Opposite the bakery, a tailor shop bustled with men trying on jackets while a woman with fabric swatches hurried in. Beside it, a perfume shop sprayed scents into the air, the aroma drifting faintly into the bakery whenever the door opened.

"You look new to this town, you don't look Scottish to me," said the bakery boy, leaning on the counter, his voice half-nosey, half-friendly, fishing for information.

"I'm from London," said Keith quietly, sipping at his tea. "I'm in search of my wife—Melicia. The woman I spoke to you about earlier."

"Ohhh, I see," said the bakery boy, raising his brows but not pressing further.

He paused, wiped his hands on his apron, then pretended to busy himself stacking a tray of rolls. A few minutes later, he returned to Keith's table, lowering his voice slightly.

"Would you need a room? I know a good motel around the corner," said the bakery boy.

Keith looked at him, wary. "Well, I would need a room to stay, I suppose. If I have to look for Melicia, it may take days. But what's in it for you? Why are you helping me out?" asked Keith, his tone curious but guarded.

The bakery boy smirked, shrugged. "Well, I'll get a commission, that's all. Nothing more."

Keith studied his face for a moment, then nodded. He could see the boy was helpful primarily, just trying to make a quick buck, not running any tricks.

"Fine," said Keith at last. "Show me this place."

The boy scribbled an address on a slip of paper and slid it across the counter. Keith picked it up, glanced at it, then stood up, picked up his luggage, and left.

The motel wasn't far. Just off Buchanan Street, tucked at the edge of a narrow bridge, behind a row of shuttered shops and glowing neon signs. The building looked tired, with its paint cracked and its name letters missing from the façade. Cars rattled over the bridge outside, their headlights cutting through the drizzle, adding to the sense of isolation.

Inside, the reception smelled faintly of damp carpet and cigarette smoke.

"One room, cash only," said the motel clerk, hardly glancing at Keith. "No hot water after midnight. You want breakfast, it's extra."

Keith frowned. "And the cleaning? The place doesn't exactly look well-kept," he said sharply, noticing the grimy skirting boards and the stain on the counter.

The clerk gave him a dead-eyed stare. "It's cheap, mate. You want the Hilton; you're on the wrong street."

Keith clenched his jaw but tossed the cash onto the counter. "Fine. Just give me the key."

The key was a bent piece of metal attached to a heavy plastic tag. When he entered the room, the air was stale. The wallpaper peeled at the corners, the carpet was threadbare, and the bathroom tap coughed out lukewarm water at best.

Keith threw his bag on the bed, sat heavily on the edge, and rubbed his face with both hands. He told himself it didn't matter. Comfort wasn't the point—finding Melicia was.

That evening, Keith decided to get some air and headed to a small café tucked at the corner of the street. The place smelled of freshly ground coffee and grilled meat — warm, inviting, alive. He took a seat by the window, the glass reflecting the city's orange streetlights flickering against the drizzle.

A young waiter approached, notepad in hand, his accent light and local. "Evenin', sir. What can I get you?"

Keith glanced at the menu, though he already knew what he wanted. "Burger and fries. And… a coffee, black."

The waiter nodded. “Comin’ right up.”

Keith leaned back and scanned the room. The café buzzed softly — couples leaning close over candlelit tables, laughing at private jokes, their fingers brushing as if the world had shrunk to the space between them. He felt an ache twist somewhere deep in his chest. Melicia would’ve liked this place, he thought. She always did love little cafés like this — the kind with peeling paint and warm light. He reached for his phone out of habit, then stopped halfway. There was no one to text anymore.

As he set the phone down, something caught his eye — a man, maybe in his late fifties, half bald, neatly dressed, sitting alone by the wall. He wasn’t eating, just nursing a drink — and staring straight at Keith. Their eyes met briefly. Keith stiffened. The man didn’t look away.

He shifted in his chair, breaking the gaze, pretending to study the menu again. Don’t engage, he told himself. Probably just some nosy local.

Then, before he could even reach for his coffee, a large, heavyset man appeared at his table and plopped into the seat across from him.

Keith blinked. “Excuse me—this table’s taken.”

The man looked around casually. “Doesn’t look like it. You’re sittin’ alone, I’m sittin’ here. Fair enough.”

Keith frowned. “There are other tables.”

The man gave a half-smile that didn’t reach his eyes. “Full house, mate. Don’t be so uptight. I’m just sharin’ a table, not your dinner.”

Keith’s patience frayed. “Sit somewhere else.”

The man only shrugged and leaned back, completely unfazed. “You’ve got issues with people, huh? No wonder you’re alone.”

Keith clenched his jaw, said nothing. His food arrived, and he ate in tight silence, eyes on his plate. Across the room, the half-bald man was still there, occasionally glancing over — not for long, but enough for Keith to notice. He kept his head down and finished quickly.

When he finally stood to leave, he felt the bulky man's eyes on his back and the faint prickling sense that he was still being watched. Outside, the night had turned colder. The air smelled faintly of rain and petrol, and every step back to the motel felt heavier than the last.

At the door, his key jammed. "Come on," he muttered, wrestling it until the lock finally gave way with a loud click.

Inside, the room felt smaller than before — the cheap wallpaper closing in, the ceiling fan groaning softly. He dropped onto the bed, exhaustion tugging at his limbs, but sleep wouldn't come.

From the next room, came bursts of laughter, thudding music — and then the unmistakable rhythm of a woman's moans, loud and unashamed.

Keith groaned, dragging a pillow over his head. "Perfect," he muttered into the fabric. "Just perfect."

The noise didn't stop. Somewhere beyond the paper-thin walls, the world carried on — loud, alive, indifferent — while he lay there in the dark, wide awake, counting the seconds until morning.

Chapter 4

Buchanan Street

Keith woke with a skull-splitting throb behind his eyes. The motel pillow might as well have been a brick wrapped in a pillowcase, and the mattress squeaked like it was auditioning for a haunted house. He rubbed his temples and sat up, groaning.

"Goodness… feels like someone's been hammering nails inside my head."

Dragging himself into the bathroom, he twisted the tap for hot water. A miserable cough of pipes, then—ice cold. He yelped as the splash hit his chest.

"Oh, come on! He swore hot water till nine!" Keith growled, staring at his watch: 8:42 a.m.

He stormed down to reception, dripping wet and wrapped in a half-buttoned shirt. The motel manager, a wiry man with a wispy moustache and a shiny fake Rolex dangling too loosely from his wrist, barely looked up from his newspaper.

Keith slapped the counter. "Mate, you said hot water till nine."

The manager sniffed, pointing at a cardboard sign taped to the wall: 'Hot Water – 6 am to 8.30 am ONLY. Management Not Responsible After.'

"That wasn't there yesterday."

"It's there now," the manager replied flatly, flipping a page.

"Convenient," Keith muttered, shivering as he stomped back to the lift.

Inside the cramped lift, the fluorescent bulb flickered as if it were about to die. As the doors slid shut, a couple squeezed in. The man smelled of stale whisky; the woman wore oversized sunglasses and a handbag that screamed Gucci, but was spelled Gucci.

"Sorry, a bit tight," Keith mumbled, hugging the wall.

The woman leaned into him, pressing closer than necessary. Her perfume was strong enough to knock out a horse.

"Y'know," she whispered in a husky Glaswegian accent, "you look like ye could use… a wee distraction. Just a quick time, for a charge."

Keith's eyes widened. "Excuse me?!"

The bloke chuckled. "Ignore her, pal. She's a bit… entrepreneurial."

Keith squirmed. "Right. Well. Not my kind of—erm—transaction, thanks." He darted out the moment the lift doors groaned open.

Outside, Glasgow's Buchanan Street was alive already: shoppers in Primark bags, students with headphones, tourists fumbling with maps. Stalls lined the corner, hawking "designer" handbags that were more Dodgy Street than Bond Street. Sellers shouted:

"Rolex! Fifty quid! Looks just like the real thing! Louis Vuitton handbags! Straight from Paris! Tenner!"

Keith smirked at the chaos. “Counterfeit city,” he muttered, shaking his head.

His eyelids sagged with exhaustion, but something inside kept him moving. He made his way back to the bakery, the smell of fresh pastries guiding him like a beacon. He ordered the same as yesterday—tea and a doughnut—before settling into his seat by the window.

The bakery was warm, humming with chatter. A pair of students debated over lecture notes, an old woman scolded her grandson for licking the sugar off a bun, and behind the counter, the barista tried to flog yesterday’s croissants as ‘vintage-style.’

Keith hardly registered the bustle around him. His tea cooled in the cup, and the croissant sat half-eaten on the plate. His gaze never left the street—tracking every passerby with a desperate, practised sharpness. Shoppers with bags, buses hissing to a stop, tourists pausing for photos—all of them blurred into background noise. None of them mattered. He was waiting for someone.

He was here for her.

His heart pounded despite the lack of sleep; his body sagged, but his mind was razor sharp. He tapped the table with his fingers, whispering to himself:

“Come on, Melicia. Just once. Walk past, give us a sign you’re real.”

Every face that passed the glass was another blow of disappointment, another reminder that he might be chasing a ghost.

And yet he waited, sipping lukewarm tea, as counterfeit handbags, knock-off Rolexes, and dodgy motel rooms faded into nothing but scenery.

He resolved to head back out and make further enquiries. Once again, he stopped passers-by, his questions growing more urgent each time. Most ignored him outright, muttering as they hurried past. "Get away, man," one snapped, brushing his shoulder. Others barely glanced at him, treating him like a madman.

Undeterred, Keith pressed on, knocking at shop doors, waving Melicia's photograph like a man possessed. Eventually, he pushed open the wooden door of a small tailor's shop, the faint jingle of the bell announcing his arrival. The air was thick with the scent of mothballs and stale fabric.

From his pocket, Keith produced the worn photograph of Melicia and slid it across the counter. "You see this woman?" he asked, his voice tight, betraying the strain he carried.

The two men behind the counter exchanged a look, one curling his lip into a mocking grin.

"What's this, eh? Lost your woman?" the first man sneered, his Italian accent thick, his English broken.

"Maybe she ran away cause you don't have money for good clothes, eh?"

Keith's jaw clenched. "Say that again."

The second man laughed, shaking his head. "Look at you—like a stray dog. You beg for a woman; you are no man. Pathetic."

A younger man lounging near the back whistled and chimed in, "Eh, maybe she's with a real man now."

Something in Keith snapped. "Better a stray dog than a pair of clowns hiding behind needles and thread. At least I don't spend my life stitching trousers while your mothers are still patching up your pride."

The laughter stopped dead. Their faces hardened, humour gone in an instant. The eldest leaned forward, his voice dropping to a cold hiss. "You don't know where you are, foreigner. This is no tailor shop. This place… family business. You spit in the wrong place."

Keith's stomach dropped. A back door creaked open. Two thick-set men stepped through—broad-shouldered, eyes hard, carrying the quiet weight of real menace. One adjusted his jacket just enough to show the glint of a knife.

"Oh, bollocks," Keith muttered under his breath—then bolted.

The shop erupted behind him in angry Italian curses as he tore through the doorway, trainers hammering against the cobbles. His breath rasped, chest burning, as he ducked between startled pedestrians. "Get him! Prendi Lui!" voices roared from behind. He risked a glance over his shoulder—four, maybe five of them giving chase. One flicked open a blade, the steel catching in the streetlight.

"Why do I always do this to myself?" Keith groaned aloud as he vaulted a stack of crates, stumbling into an alley.

He burst onto the main road—just as headlights blazed into his eyes. A sleek black Porsche came tearing round the corner, engine snarling like an animal. The gang skidded to a halt, shielding their faces as the car swung sideways with a screech, tyres spitting smoke.

Keith froze, certain he was about to be flattened. But the passenger door snapped open. "Get in!" a woman's voice cut through the chaos, sharp as glass.

Keith didn't think—he just threw himself inside, slamming the door. The Porsche roared forward, leaving the Italians coughing in a cloud of exhaust and fury.

His chest heaved, heart pounding in his ears. Slowly, he turned to face the driver.

His breath caught. "Melicia…?"

But she was not the Melicia he remembered—no soft dresses, no easy laugh in their small kitchen. This Melicia was something else entirely. Black leather trousers, a fitted jacket hugging her frame, a silk scarf knotted neatly at her throat. Dark glasses masked her eyes, but the set of her jaw was enough.

She didn't look at him, hands steady on the wheel as she tore through the streets. "Buckle up."

He sat frozen, trying to reconcile the woman he once knew with the stranger now rescuing him.

Back on the pavement, the Italians cursed and waved their hands. And across the street, half-hidden by a doorway, the bakery boy stood wide-eyed, watching it all unfold.

Melicia eased off the accelerator and pulled towards the kerb, the Porsche purring into uneasy silence. She slipped her sunglasses from her face, resting both hands on the wheel before turning, her eyes catching his in a flicker of guilt and defiance.

Keith sat rigid, jaw locked, Adam's apple bobbing like he'd swallowed a stone. He didn't know where to start, whether to rage, beg, or sit there in silence—but the words broke free regardless. "I'm listening. Go on then. Tell me. Why did you leave me? Why did you vanish? And for God's sake, why pretend you were dead? Who does that?"

Melicia's voice was calm, low, with a teasing edge. "Do you remember how we met?"

Keith gave a short, ragged laugh—half cough, half protest. "Remember? Melicia, how could I forget? That was the most ridiculous, unbelievable day of my life. The best day… but utterly mad. You—you came tearing into my life like some runaway actress. You bumped into me, and before I even knew your name, you kissed me. Right there on the pavement in front of half of Hamburg folks!"

Melicia's mouth curved, amusement flickering. "You make it sound like I broke the law."

"A law? People don't just go about kissing strangers in broad daylight, in front of a bus queue! Do you have any idea what happened after you disappeared into the crowd?"

Her eyebrow arched, her voice lilting with challenge. "Do tell."

Keith flung his hands up, almost strangling himself in the seatbelt. "I stood there like a complete idiot! An old lady clutched her handbag as if I were some serial kisser roaming the streets. A builder across the road whistled and shouted, 'Go on, lad!' The bus driver laughed so hard he nearly knocked over a cyclist. And me? I just stood there with your lipstick smeared across my face, looking like a clown who'd lost the plot."

He shook his head, eyes rolling with dramatic misery. "For the next three days, I came back to the same spot, same time, waiting for you. I even slapped myself for it—thought I was losing my mind. Eventually, I gave up. Too good to be true, I told myself. What would a nobody like me ever deserve with a woman like you?"

His voice dropped, gentler now, as his eyes flicked toward her. "But then it happened. I'd just wrapped up my German forum sessions, on my way home, minding my own business. And suddenly—you appeared. Bold as brass, you slipped your hand into mine. I looked up, and there you were. I mean—things like that don't happen to an ordinary bloke like me. Never. But you—" he shook his head lightly, almost in disbelief, "you did."

Melicia leaned in slightly, her smile warmer now, eyes glistening with something unspoken. She reached across, running her fingers through his hair in a slow, teasing gesture. “You talk too much, Keith. And that’s what I like about you.”

He froze, searching her face, but she only smirked. “Well, you’re here now. That’s what counts. I’ll explain everything later.”

She flicked the ignition, the Porsche purring back to life, and pulled away from the kerb.

Keith stared at her profile as the streetlights streaked across the glass. “Whose car is this, anyway?” he asked, suspicion edging his voice.

Melicia’s lips pressed into a smile, but she offered no reply. Instead, she drove them out of town, leaving the city lights shrinking in the rear-view until they reached a quiet block of condominiums on the outskirts.

Inside, she dropped the keys into a bowl by the door and vanished into the bedroom without a word. Keith lingered, scanning the place like a hawk—checking every corner for signs of another man. Nothing. No shoes by the door. No jacket slung over a chair. No scent of cologne. He exhaled, sagging into the sofa.

Moments later, Melicia reappeared—her hair down now, tumbling across her shoulders, her silhouette softened into a slung vest top and loose boxer shorts.

Keith blinked. She was at once a stranger and a wife.

“I would like you to meet Joshua,” she said.

Keith shot upright, eyes darting. “What—who?!” he barked, half-panicked, searching the flat for shadows.

Melicia stifled a laugh and bent behind the sofa. From the corner, she scooped up a lazy white Persian cat, its tail flicking as if bored by the drama. “This is Joshua. My cat.”

Keith stared, dumbfounded. Then, almost reluctantly, he took the cat from her arms. To his surprise, the creature purred instantly, leaning into his hand. “Joshua likes you,” Melicia said with a grin. “He doesn’t usually like men.”

Keith narrowed his eyes, clutching the cat. “Men? Are there any men in your life, Melicia?” he asked, voice rising hysterically.

She didn’t answer. Instead, she pivoted. “How did you find me?”

Keith smirked faintly, still absently stroking the cat in his lap. “Credit goes to Ryan, really. You remember him—the social geek. He spotted you in the background of some influencer’s Instagram reel. That was all I needed. A few sleepless nights, a bit of digging, and… here I am.”

Melicia tilted her head, amusement flickering in her eyes. “Smarter than I thought,” she teased, lips curling into a sly smile.

Keith puffed up a little, pride leaking into his voice. “What were you running from, Melicia? You looked like you’d seen a ghost.” His tone sharpened, hoping to catch her off guard.

Melicia’s grin widened. “Shopping. That’s all. Someone didn’t appreciate my choices and decided to chase me.”

Keith, sprawled on the armchair, snorted. “You mean you shoplifted.”

“Not entirely,” Melicia replied smoothly, unbothered. “I paid for most of it.” Her voice was slow, deliberate, but carried no hint of guilt.

Keith arched a brow. “So, you’re a thief now?”

She waved the accusation away with a flick of her hand. “Oh, don’t be dramatic. I just… can’t help myself sometimes. A woman has her needs. A little jewellery here and there—what’s the harm?”

Keith opened his mouth to reply—but the sharp trill of the doorbell cut through the room.

The sound cut through the flat like a blade.

Melicia froze, then silently pressed a finger to her lips. She crept towards the door on her toes, careful not to let the floorboards creak. Leaning in, she peered through the peephole.

Her shoulders stiffened.

Keith whispered hoarsely, “Who is it?”

She turned her head slowly, her expression unreadable. “It’s Sunny. The bakery boy.”

Melicia opened the door and let Sunny in. The boy shuffled inside, eyes darting about the flat until they landed on Keith. For a moment, the two just stared at each other, strangers bound by some unspoken curiosity. Keith gave a hesitant half-wave, the kind one gives when caught in the wrong room at the wrong time.

Sunny blinked, then offered the same awkward salute before thrusting a folded slip of paper into Melicia’s hand.

Her eyes skimmed the words, and her smile collapsed in an instant. Her jaw tightened; the room seemed to shrink around her. She dismissed Sunny with a curt nod, and the boy slipped out, silent as he’d arrived.

Keith leaned forward on the sofa. “What was that about?”

But Melicia didn’t answer. She clutched the paper and walked into the bedroom without a word, shutting the door softly behind her.

Keith stood, half-ready to knock, half-ready to barge in. He lingered outside her door, hand raised, knuckles hovering just above the wood. But his gut told him she wouldn't talk. Not now. With a frustrated sigh, he slumped back onto the sofa and lay down, staring into the dark until sleep crept over him.

When he stirred, the flat was hushed and dim. Streetlight glow leaked in through the blinds, striping the walls in pale gold. Melicia stood above him.

Keith's breath caught. She was dressed in a cream slip gown that shimmered with each movement. Around her neck hung the silver pendant he'd given her on their first anniversary. She looked impossibly elegant—like a dream slipping back into reality.

"Come on," she whispered. "Let's go out. Just you and me. Like old times."

Keith rubbed his eyes and groaned. "Old times? The old times when you staged a death scene and scarpered?"

But he was already on his feet, disappearing into the bathroom. Three minutes later, he re-emerged, hair wet, face freshly splashed, still tugging his sleeves into place.

They stepped out into the night. The air carried a bite, lamps buzzing faintly overhead. Melicia slipped her hand into his. Keith froze for half a second, then let it happen.

They strolled aimlessly, peering into shopfronts like tourists. Keith exaggerated his commentary on everything they saw. "Look at that mannequin—standing like it's got chronic back pain. And that scarf—what, five hundred quid? For something you could knit while drunk?"

Melicia burst out laughing, the sound rolling down the quiet street. She tilted her head back, her hair catching the glow of the lamps. For a while, they slipped into an easy rhythm—laughing, pointing, teasing—like nothing had ever broken between them.

They ended up at a tiny family-run restaurant tucked into the corner of a converted townhouse. Inside was warmth: mismatched lamps, four wobbly tables, and the smell of garlic and bread clinging to the air. The owner's wife brought them steaming bowls of pasta and wine in scratched tumblers.

Keith watched her in the soft light, drinking her in as if she might vanish if he blinked. Finally, he leaned closer.

"Melicia… why? Why did you leave me? Why pretend to be dead?"

Her fork froze mid-air. Her eyes softened, wet with a flicker of honesty, but she smothered it with a brittle smile. "Try the tiramisu. It's supposed to be heavenly."

Keith clenched his jaw but said nothing. Not here. Not now.

When they left, the streets had quieted. Melicia clung to his hand tighter than before, glancing over her shoulder every few minutes. Keith noticed. He felt it too—the prickling sense of being followed. But she masked it with a steady stride, pulling him along.

By the time they reached her flat, the tension was back, heavy and sharp. She unlocked the door, stepped inside, and turned with forced lightness. "You can stay tonight. It's late."

Keith nodded, though his mind swirled.

Minutes later, she emerged from the bedroom, holding out a bundle of clothes. "Here. This is all I've got for you."

Keith unfolded them—a long t-shirt and loose pyjamas, both unmistakably hers. He raised an eyebrow. "Oh, well, better than manly wears."

Her smirk said otherwise.

Keith returned from the bathroom wearing them, the t-shirt nearly swallowing him, the pyjamas clinging in all the wrong places. He strutted into the living room with his best catwalk impression. "Well? Paris Fashion Week ready? Or more… charity shop chic?"

Melicia collapsed onto the sofa laughing, tears at the corners of her eyes. "You look ridiculous."

"Better ridiculous than naked in your living room," he shot back, grinning.

Their laughter melted into a quiet warmth. They stood close, too close. Keith brushed a strand of hair from her face, and before he could stop himself, he kissed her. For one beautiful moment, she kissed him back—slow, aching, familiar.

She drew back; her voice edged with steel. "Keith… don't." She wanted to yield, to stay in that moment, but something held her fast. Her mind was elsewhere, burdened, as if carrying a weight too heavy to set down.

"Come with me," he whispered. "Back home. We can fix it. We can fix us."

She shook her head, her smile fading. "Keith, I was bored. Don't you see? Two and a half years of marriage felt like a prison. I wanted more. Needed more. And you—you weren't enough."

Thewordshitlikeablade.Keithstaggeredback,colourdrainingfromhisface. "Not enough? After everything—"

"I faked my death so you'd move on."

The silence that followed was heavier than any scream. Melicia turned and disappeared into the bedroom, the door shutting with a soft, merciless click.

Keith sank onto the sofa in his borrowed pyjamas, staring at the ceiling as the night stretched on. Sleep came in shallow snatches, haunted and jagged.

At first light, he rose quietly, gathered his things, and left. The door clicked shut behind him—soft as a sigh, final as a grave.

Melicia stirred awake the next morning, stretching across the bed. The other side was cold. Empty. She sat up, blinking against the pale light slipping in through the curtains. For a moment, she half expected to see Keith sprawled on the sofa in her oversized T-shirt, snoring lightly. But the couch was bare.

Her heart sank. Slowly, she lowered herself onto the cushions, burying her face in her hands. She sat there in silence, shoulders trembling, knowing he had gone without a word.

Meanwhile, Keith's cab pulled up outside the shabby motel. The neon sign buzzed faintly above the doorway. From across the street, the two burly men from the tailor's shop clocked him instantly. They stepped out, blocking the pavement with their sheer size.

Keith stopped dead, his hands still in his pockets. His face was unreadable, cold. He locked eyes with them, refusing to flinch.

The bigger of the two muttered, "You've got some nerve, mate." Keith didn't flinch. He just stared back, hollow and exhausted, as if nothing they did could possibly be worse than what he'd already been through.

The men stared back, but something in his eyes made them falter. Whatever they saw there wasn't anger—it was something sharper, heavier. They backed away without another word.

From the corner bakery, young Sunny peered out through the window, recognising Keith immediately. His brow furrowed, lips pursed, but he said nothing. Just watched as Keith disappeared inside the motel.

Keith went straight to his room. No hesitation. He tossed his belongings into his bag, zipped it shut, and left. At the front desk, he slid the key across to the manager along with the balance of his rent.

"Checking out early?" the manager asked, raising a brow.

Keith gave a thin smile. "Checking out permanently."

No more was said. He stepped outside, waved down a cab, and was gone.

At the airport, Keith managed to secure a seat on a flight leaving in a couple of hours. He lingered in a coffee shop, staring into a cup he'd long since drained, absently stirring the melted dregs as though they might give him something new. His phone rested in his palm, screen glowing with fragments of another life—him and Melicia laughing at a fairground, sunburnt on a beach, her face pressed to his shoulder. He swiped through them slowly, jaw set hard, each image cutting deeper than the last.

Around him, the terminal pulsed with noise. A family wrestled with suitcases that looked ready to explode, snapping at each other while blocking the walkway. Businesspeople barked into their phones like drill sergeants. Nearby, a pack of children tore through the seating area, weaving between chairs, shrieking like wild puppies. One of them collided with his leg, nearly knocking the phone from his hand. Their mother didn't even look up from hers.

Keith exhaled sharply through his nose, muttering under his breath, "Brilliant. Just what I need."

Fate tested him more; those same children ended up not only on his flight, but in the seats directly beside him.

The moment the plane took off, chaos erupted—kicking seats, tugging at the in-flight magazine, and shrieking with laughter. One of them even managed to spill orange juice on Keith's sleeve.

He pressed the call button, jaw tight.

The air hostess leaned down politely. "Yes, sir?"

"Any chance," Keith asked, voice strained, "that you've got a spare seat somewhere—anywhere—else on this plane?"

She offered him a sympathetic smile that didn't reach her eyes. "I'm afraid we're full tonight."

Keith groaned. "Of course you are. Full to bursting—with gremlins."

The hostess stifled a laugh. "I'll see if I can get you some extra napkins."

For the next few hours, Keith endured a symphony of shrieks, thuds, and the endless sound of crisps being crunched right in his ear. He muttered curses at his luck, at Melicia, at life itself.

"Perfect ending to a perfect lousy trip," he said to no one in particular, drawing a few odd looks from nearby passengers.

By the time the wheels hit the runway back home, he looked like a man who had survived a warzone. He shuffled off the plane, hair mussed, shirt wrinkled, clutching his bag as though it had been through the trenches with him.

Chapter 5

A Thorn In My Side

The next morning, Keith returned to work. He slid into his chair without a word, ignoring the curious glances from his colleagues.

"Back from holiday, then?" one of them asked cheerfully.

Keith gave a curt nod; his eyes fixed on his desk.

"So… how was it?" another ventured.

He didn't look up. "You don't want to know."

And that was that. He buried himself in his work, shutting out their questions and everything else.

On reaching home from work, Keith found Ryan leaning against the wall outside his doorstep. "Oi, mate! How did it go?" he called, grinning.

Keith scowled. "Don't you have something better to do?" he muttered, shoving the front door open. Ryan slipped in behind him without a word.

"I was dumped," Keith said flatly, flopping into the armchair. "She faked her own death just to get away from me. Apparently, I'm the most boring man alive."

Ryan crouched beside him, trying to soften the blow. "Now, now… maybe she had her reasons."

Keith let out a humourless laugh. "Yeah, her reason was dumping me and moving on!"

Ryan waved a hand, eager. "Right, listen. Forget her for one night. Let's get out—clubbing, drinks, music. Shake it off, yeah?"

Keith groaned, hesitating. Ryan didn't wait for an answer, yanking him towards the door. "Come on! You don't even need to change," he added, grinning mischievously.

Despite every instinct screaming at him to walk away, Keith went along. Ryan was already buzzing, drumming the steering wheel with his fingers as he filled the car with rapid-fire chatter, half-jokes, half-nonsense. Keith barely listened. His eyes stayed fixed on the blur of streetlights, the city pressing in closer as they drew nearer to the thumping neon glow ahead.

The nightclub announced itself long before they saw it. The bass was a physical thing, a low, relentless throb that shook the pavement, rattled his ribcage, and made his teeth vibrate. The queue outside was a parade of sequins, short skirts, leather jackets, and bravado. Inside, the air was thick—alcohol, sweat, perfume, and the faint tang of smoke clinging to everything. Lights strobed in jagged blues and reds, slicing across writhing bodies like warning beacons in a storm.

Ryan threw himself into the crowd as though he'd been waiting his whole life for this one night. He was laughing, high-fiving strangers, limbs flailing in rhythm—or perhaps completely out of rhythm—with the music. He looked ridiculous and joyous at once.788

Keith, by contrast, slunk into the shadows at the edge of the club. He nursed a whiskey on the rocks, watching the ice melt, trying his hardest to be invisible. He wasn't built for this scene anymore. If he ever was.

That's when she appeared.

She slid into view like smoke, hips swaying, her silhouette framed in neon. Dark hair fell in a loose curtain over one shoulder, a glint of silver winking against her throat. She leaned in close, the scent of jasmine cutting through the acrid cocktail of the club, her lips almost brushing his ear.

"Fancy a dance?" she purred, voice lilting, eyes glittering with the promise of trouble.

Keith glanced at her, forced a polite half-smile, and shook his head. "No, thank you. I'm fine on my own." His tone was clipped, his eyes deliberately on his glass. He was determined not to notice the low neckline of her dress, the curve of her body pressed too close.

Her pout was interrupted by the sudden arrival of another figure. A thin man in a navy suit. Not stylish, thin—gaunt, like the suit was carrying him rather than the other way around. His hair was immaculately parted; his shoes polished within an inch of their lives. He perched beside Keith with the incredible precision of someone who spent more time in front of a mirror than in the real world.

"Do you like my girlfriend?" the man asked smoothly, his voice syrupy sweet, yet edged with menace.

Keith raised an eyebrow, already exhausted. "I couldn't care less, mate. Let me be. I'm here for the drink, not the company."

But the man leaned closer, his smirk growing. "Well… my girlfriend seems to like you. And if she fancies a man, I make sure she has the pleasure she seeks. Don't you think that's… fair?"

Keith choked on his whiskey, coughing out a laugh. "What? Are you serious? I said Stay away. I'm not interested."

Just then, Ryan, wobbling from too many shots, noticed the tension. He staggered over, sweat glistening on his forehead. "Oi! Oi, what's happening here then?!"

The suited man turned, grin widening. "It's simple, mate. My girlfriend likes your friend here. And me? I like to make her happy. So why not let him… indulge?"

Keith groaned, pinching the bridge of his nose. "Indulge? I came here to drink, not audition for the lunatic fringe."

Ryan put an arm around Keith's shoulders, leaning in with drunken urgency. "Keith, mate. Just go with it. Trust me. I'll sort it."

Keith gave him a withering glare. "Go with it? Are you mad? These two are barking."

Ryan, eyes glassy but insistent, whispered, "Trust me. Please. Just follow upstairs. I'll handle the rest."

Keith stared at him, incredulous. "Follow them upstairs? Into what? Some pervy honeymoon suite?"

Ryan grinned like a guilty schoolboy. "Something like that. Come on."

Against every ounce of reason, Keith found himself trailing them. The four of them piled into a lift, the doors closing with a metallic hunk. The confined space reeked of perfume, sweat, and cheap cologne. The woman giggled, deliberately brushing against Keith. The suited man hummed a tuneless melody, smug as sin. Ryan winked at Keith, though his drunken sway made the wink look more like a twitch.

Keith's stomach churned. This was a mistake. A monumental mistake.

Upstairs, the room was dimly lit, plush carpet muffling their footsteps. The woman leaned against the doorframe, swirling a glass of red wine, eyes gleaming with playful intent. "More drinks?" she offered, voice like honeyed smoke.

Keith waved her off. "No, thanks. Really, I'm—"

But the combination of dim lights, thumping music from below, and Ryan's insistence made resistance pointless. The drinks were poured, hands grazed, laughs that were supposed to be innocent tinged with something else.

Hours later, Keith's skull throbbed like someone was hammering nails into it. He woke in stages, first the muffled hum of the air-con, then the ache in his gut, then the realisation that the hotel room was unnervingly quiet.

He forced his eyes open. Ryan lay sprawled on the carpet, snoring faintly, his shirt half-unbuttoned and his hair sticking out in every direction, like a hedgehog that had lost a fight with a tumble dryer.

Keith groaned, dragged himself upright, and immediately clocked the disaster. The bedside table was bare. No wallet. No phone. His pockets were lighter than air.

"Brilliant," he muttered, massaging the bridge of his nose. "Absolutely brilliant."

Ryan stirred, groaning. "Whassat?" He blinked blearily. "Why are you glaring at me?"

Keith jabbed a finger at him. "Because you did this. You dragged me into this circus. And now? We've been cleaned out."

Ryan sat up, scratching his head, looking confused. "What, you mean…?" He patted his own trousers, then his jacket. His eyes widened. "Oh bollocks. They've taken my wallet. My phone. My—" He froze. "My car keys."

Keith threw his arms up. "Of course they did! They've stripped us clean. My pockets are emptier than your promises. I think we've been roofied!"

Ryan winced, stumbling to his feet. "… it seemed like a good idea at the time, alright?"

"A good idea?" Keith barked, voice cracking. "I'm hungover, robbed, and I've just spent the night in a cheap hotel suite with you. Nothing about this is a good idea!"

They staggered downstairs, out into the dim morning light. The pavement reeked of stale beer and cigarette butts. Keith scanned the street—the parking bay where Ryan's car should have been sat ominously empty.

Keith turned, jaw tight. "Don't tell me—"

Ryan gave a pitiful shrug. "Gone."

Keith clenched his fists. "You deserve this…"

Ryan grabbed his arm before he could spiral further. "Look, we go to the police. That's it. We file a report and keep it on record. Come on. Keep your shirt on."

At the police station, the stale smell of burnt coffee mixed with disinfectant hit Keith like a wall—sharp, bitter, and unmistakably familiar. Phones rang in uneven rhythms, keys clattered against metal desks, and somewhere in the corner, an officer laughed far too loudly at a joke no one else reacted to. The desk officer didn't even bother lifting his head when Keith walked in.

But someone else did.

"Keith?"

The voice cut cleanly through the low hum of the room.

Keith turned. Officer Leann stood a few steps away, clipboard tucked to her chest, her expression flickering between surprise, suspicion, and something eerily close to pity. Her boots clicked in a slow, deliberate rhythm as she approached.

"What brings you here?" she asked, tilting her head as her eyes moved over him—his wrinkled shirt, the exhaustion etched under his eyes, the faint smoky scent still clinging to him. Then she added with a stern but almost teasing edge, "What have you gotten yourself into this time?"

Keith let out a humourless breath. "You can thank my friend for that."

Leannraisedaneyebrow,butbeforeshecouldpressfurther,hertonesoftened. "How are you holding up after… the accident?" That last word hovered gently, like she was afraid it might shatter him if spoken too hard.

Keith swallowed, his throat tightening.

Then came the question he dreaded, disguised as casual curiosity: "You still haven't claimed your wife's insurance. Any reason for the delay? Most men I know would've jumped—it's a huge amount."

Another blow. His jaw clenched. A muscle in his cheek twitched.

Before he could speak, Ryan blurted out—far too loud, far too honest—

"She's alive!"

The entire front desk turned. Even the old coffee machine sputtered as if reacting to the outburst.

Keith snapped toward Ryan so fast the air seemed to whip between them. His glare was lethal.

"Ryan."

One word. A warning. A threat. A plea.

Ryan wilted, pale and sweaty, wringing his hands like a schoolboy caught cheating. "I—I mean… not literally alive. Spiritually? Maybe?"

Keith let out a strained, forced laugh and turned back to Leann. "Ignore him. He's drunk. Or hungover. Or both." Then, with a bitter grin sharp enough to draw blood, he added, "As for the insurance— I'll get to it. She's dead to me, that's for sure."

Leann's eyebrow rose a fraction. Just enough to show she noticed. Not enough to accuse.

"Right," she said, pulling out her pen. "Let's talk about your theft report. Start from the top."

Keith rubbed his temples, a sigh escaping him. His voice came out low and drained. But Ryan—oh, Ryan—launched into a chaotic narrative involving "a skinny bloke in a suit, two free tequilas, and then suddenly nothing was free anymore." His hands flew wildly, like he was conducting a drunken orchestra.

Leann scribbled everything down without changing expression. When she finally set her pen aside, she said, too casually, "I'll drive you home."

Keith blinked. "That's… not standard procedure."

She gave a slight, knowing smirk. "Consider it community care."

But beneath that smirk burned curiosity—bright and relentless. Keith's tone. His dodging. The insurance. The way Ryan nearly folded under the slightest pressure. Her instincts screamed that something was off. Badly off.

The drive home was thick with silence. The radio crackled static, Ryan hummed tunelessly in the backseat like a broken karaoke machine, and Keith sat rigid, staring out the window as though the darkness outside might swallow the truth whole. His breaths were tight, controlled.

Leann kept glancing at him through the rear-view mirror. The twitch in his jaw. The restless tapping of his fingers against his knee. The way he refused—even accidentally—to meet her eyes.

At his doorstep, Keith stepped out and closed the door gently, as if slamming it might reveal something he couldn't afford.

"Thanks for the lift," he muttered.

"No trouble," Leann replied, voice smooth—almost too soft.

But her gaze lingered on him. Sharp. Calculating. Relentless. Watching. Measuring. Waiting for the cracks to show.

Keith collapsed onto the sofa, every muscle protesting, limbs heavy as though weighted by lead. Ryan flopped down beside him, groaning.

"Never… never again," Ryan muttered, voice muffled against the cushions. "No more women in nightclubs. Ever. I swear."

Keith let out a dry chuckle. "You've said that before. Only this time it might actually stick."

Ryan dragged himself to the bedroom, muttering under his breath, "I swear, if one more girl tries to drag me upstairs—" The moment his head hit the pillow, he was out cold.

Keith pulled a blanket over his face, letting out a long, defeated groan. The night had been chaotic, humiliating, and absurd. And yet, grimly, he thought, he was still alive to tell the tale. Ryan slept sprawled across the couch, one arm dangling over the edge, snoring softly.

Hours of deep, exhausted sleep passed before a sharp knock shattered the silence, echoing through the apartment. Keith stirred, one eye peeking out from under the blanket, but it was Ryan who reacted first.

"If that's the postman again—" Ryan muttered, sleep-heavy, and swung the door open without hesitation.

Everything happened in an instant. A brutal, unexpected blow struck the side of his head. Stars exploded behind his vision. Before he could even cry out, a rough sack was yanked over him, tightening mercilessly at the neck. Panic surged as he thrashed unthinkingly, fingers clawing at the coarse fabric, but the grip of unseen hands was unyielding.

"Mmph! Hey! Let go!" His muffled shouts bounced back at him from the sack.

Two tall, broad-shouldered men, faces hidden beneath hooded jackets, bundled him like a rag doll. Ryan swung his legs, kicked out blindly, but they were too strong. "Oi! What the—let me go!" His voice cracked in panic as they dragged him swiftly down the corridor.

Out through the back exit they went, the cold night air hitting him like a wave. They carried him to the dimly lit basement car park. The smell of oil and damp concrete made him gag. Without ceremony, they dumped him into the boot of a waiting black saloon, slammed it shut, and the tyres screeched as the car sped into the night.

Keith woke later, disoriented. His head throbbed, and the room spun. His house phone buzzed insistently beside him—it was his office colleague. "Where are you? It's nearly noon!"

He groaned, fumbling, "I… I'm… alright. Just… running a bit late."

Blinking against the dull morning light, Keith looked around his bedroom. Ryan was nowhere to be seen.

"Must've gone home," he muttered, shrugging off the unease. But unease still gnawed at him as he swung his legs, each movement slow, heavy, and reluctant.

He pulled on a shirt, shoved his tie crookedly around his neck, and grabbed his bag. "Great… late already. Boss is going to have my head."

By the time he burst out the door and onto the street, his heart was racing, a mix of panic, adrenaline, and residual confusion. The night's chaos had followed him into the day, and Keith knew one thing for sure—nothing about today was going to be normal.

Chapter 6

Bagged And Baffled

Keith had buried himself in the monotony of his workday when his phone buzzed on the desk. Unknown number. He hesitated, then answered.

"Hello?" His voice was cautious.

At first, there was only silence. He thought the line had gone dead—then came a voice, soft yet unmistakably chilling.

"Hi."

His heart jolted. It was Melicia.

Before he could respond, she continued, her words quick, deliberate: "Meet me at the same place I picked you up."

The line cut. Dead silence.

Keith lowered the phone slowly, his pulse hammering, a tight knot coiling in his stomach. This wasn't some random call. Melicia was orchestrating something—but was it serious, or some cruel joke? He shook his head, trying to steady himself, then wandered into the pantry, grabbed a glass of water, and drank it in slow, deliberate sips, hoping it would wash away the sudden surge of panic.

Meanwhile, on the outskirts of Glasgow, beyond wrought-iron gates and a drive that cut through acres of dark woodland, loomed a mansion that seemed more fortress than home. Its grey stone walls bore the weight of centuries, its windows no more than narrow slits, watching like hostile eyes. Even the air around it felt oppressive, heavy with secrets.

In the attic, dust clung to every beam. The scent of old tobacco and damp wood lingered, while a single bulb dangled from the ceiling, swaying and casting crooked shadows along the walls. Melicia sat bound to a chair, her wrists rubbed raw by the coarse rope. Her once-pristine hair now fell in untidy waves about her face, the strain etched into her features.

Across from her stood Van Jeans, towering, his tailored suit pristine despite the rot of the attic around them. His voice was hard steel, his stare sharper still.

"For your sake, Melicia," he said coldly, each word deliberate and heavy, "he had better turn up."

Her chin tilted upward, eyes sparking with defiance even as her body betrayed a faint tremor. "I told you—he means nothing to me. I dumped him."

Van's lips twisted into a bitter smile; his tone laced with venom. "Poor bloke. Out of all the men you chewed up and spat out, he lasted the longest. Made me jealous, I'll admit. You got rid of me in a month—always an excuse ready. A headache, an upset stomach, 'girly troubles'… anything to keep me at arm's length. And then you stole from me on top of it."

Melicia shook her head, her voice taut but steady. "Leave him out of this. I'll return what's yours. I don't have it now, but I'll get it back to you."

Van let out a harsh, disbelieving laugh. "You? Return it? Don't make me laugh. You're a con, Melicia. That's all you've ever been." His eyes narrowed to slits, calculating. "What did you see in him, eh? A translator? Hardly dripping with money. What could you possibly have wanted—unless you meant to bleed him dry too?"

Her jaw set. "With Keith? No. I just needed a breather. I was tired of the chase. When I got bored, I dumped him too."

For the briefest moment, something flickered across Van's otherwise impassive face—hesitation, doubt, or perhaps something dangerously close to hurt. Then it hardened again.

"Same old Melicia," he sneered.

He spun towards the attic door, where two of his men loitered like chastised schoolboys. His fury ripped out in an instant. "And you two!" His roar filled the cramped space. "You got the wrong man!"

One of the goons threw up his hands, stammering. "Boss, he was the one who opened the door! We thought it was him—honest!"

The other nodded furiously, sweat gleaming on his brow. "How were we to know someone else was kipping there?"

Next to Melicia, Ryan sat tied to a chair of his own, his head spinning, utterly confused. "I told your lot they'd nabbed the wrong bloke," he croaked, wriggling against the ropes. "They didn't listen."

Melicia turned her head slightly, her voice calm despite the fear in her eyes. "Don't panic," she whispered.

Van's rage snapped like a whip. He drew his pistol in a blur, aiming it squarely at the two men. "One order. One bloody order! And you still manage to cock it up!" His finger twitched on the trigger.

The men bolted, stumbling over one another as they scrambled down the attic stairs, boots clattering in blind panic. Van didn't fire—but the silence he left behind was almost worse.

Turning back to Melicia, his voice dropped to a dangerous calm. "Keith comes to me, one way or another. He's collateral now. The only leverage I need to make sure you bring back what you stole."

With that, Van slipped his pistol back into its holster and left the attic, slamming the heavy door. One burly guard remained behind, leaning against the wall, arms folded, watching them like a hawk.

Melicia's heart clenched, though her face stayed composed, masking the dread twisting inside her.

Ryan, pale and wide-eyed, finally found his voice. "So… you're the woman who broke his heart. Thought you were dead."

Her head turned slowly, her glare cutting into him. "Don't act clever," she said icily. "You don't know a thing."

Miles away, Keith returned to his desk, still reeling from the call. Her voice—Melicia's—echoed in his mind. Impossible, yet undeniable. The words gripped him like a vice: "Meet me at the same place I picked you up."

But something in her tone had been wrong. Urgent. Frantic. Desperate. Not the Melicia he remembered.

His chest tightened, his breath shallow. He shoved back his chair, the scrape loud enough to draw stares from around the office.

“Keith? Are you alright?” a colleague asked as he strode past.

“Family emergency,” he muttered, his voice hoarse, eyes fixed on the exit. He didn’t slow. He didn’t look back.

At home, Keith moved with restless urgency, tearing through drawers and stuffing a bag with whatever he could reach—shirts, jeans, his wallet, passport, and anything that might be helpful. His hands shook, clumsy in their haste.

“What have you done now, Melicia?” he whispered into the silence, his words heavy with a mixture of dread and longing.

Before stepping out, Keith crouched by the small glass tank in the corner where Turbo, his pet turtle, floated lazily in the water. He tapped the rim gently, and the little creature blinked up at him, slow and unbothered.

“You’ll be alright, mate,” Keith murmured, his voice softer than he intended, almost as if he needed to hear it himself. He sprinkled in an extra handful of pellets, watching them scatter across the surface before sinking into it.

Without wasting another second, he straightened, grabbed his jacket, and yanked the door open. The slam echoed down the hall as he rushed out, taking the stairs two at a time, not even glancing at the waiting lift.

He tried to reach Ryan, but the phone was off. “Where is he when I need him the most?” grumbled Keith.

An hour later, he was slumped into one of the unforgiving plastic chairs at the airport departure gate, staring at the floor tiles but seeing nothing. The atmosphere clawed at him. Every burst of laughter, the tap of hurried footsteps, even the sharp cough of a stranger, made his head twitch round. Paranoia gripped him. He could feel eyes on him—though no one was there.

When the boarding call finally echoed through the terminal, Keith stood, his grip tightening on the strap of his bag. "Right," he murmured under his breath, the words barely audible. "Let's end this."

As the engines thundered to life and the plane clawed its way into the night sky, Keith leaned back into the seat, heart pounding. It was Melicia. That much was real. But what had she been dragged into? And who—waiting in the shadows of Glasgow—was pulling the strings?

Keith stepped out of the arrivals gate, the Glasgow evening wrapping him in a damp chill. The sky was that heavy grey that seemed to have hung over the city for centuries. He hailed a cab, climbed in, and muttered the address—the place Melicia had told him. No questions asked.

The ride dragged in silence, only the faint squeak of the wipers as drizzle smeared across the windscreen. By the time the cab pulled up, the streets were thinning out, lamplight painting long shadows across the pavement. Keith paid, hoisted his bag, and stood there exactly where she'd picked him up before—same cracked pavement. The same rusted lamppost flickered, as if it couldn't quite decide whether to give up or not.

He scanned the passers-by, restless. A woman with a pram. A lad on a bike, earbuds in. But no Melicia. His heart thudded as he waited, bag at his feet, half-hoping and half-dreading she would actually appear. The last time they'd spoken, she'd made it painfully clear—she wanted him out of her life. So, what was this? A second chance? A trap? Or just another one of her games?

Headlights cut across his thoughts. A sleek black Vell fire van rolled up to the kerb, humming low like a predator purring. The rear door clicked open, but it wasn't Melicia who emerged.

A bald man stepped out, broad as a wardrobe, his expression unreadable. Keith's gut twisted—he recognised him. A few days ago, at that restaurant, this same bloke had been sitting in the corner, eyes fixed on him like a hawk. Keith had brushed it off then, chalking it up to paranoia. But now? Now it made sense.

"So, I was being followed," Keith muttered to himself, stomach knotting. "And here I thought I was just irresistible company."

The man walked right up to him—no small talk, no hesitation—planted heavy hands-on Keith's shoulders and steered him towards the van.

Keith stiffened, his voice cracking out nervously. "Hang on. I usually like to know someone's name before I get shoved into their car. Bit of a quirk of mine."

The bald man said nothing, just pressed him forward with the sort of silent authority that didn't need words.

Keith bent awkwardly to scoop up his bag. "Right then," he muttered, climbing in. "Into the mystery van with the stranger it is. Nothing suspicious about this at all."

The door slammed shut behind him, the sound echoing like a vault locking.

Inside, the air was heavy with the scent of leather and a faintly chemical odour. Keith sat stiff, clutching his bag in his lap, his mind whirling.

Why him? Why Melicia? Why Glasgow, of all places?

He had no answers—just the sinking feeling that whatever this was, he was already in far deeper than he'd ever meant to go.

The black Vell fire van rolled to a stop before the looming gates of the mansion, purring like some expensive jungle cat. The iron gates creaked open with theatrical menace, though Keith suspected it was just in dire need of over-oiling. The van glided up the gravel drive and stopped in the shadow of the grand estate.

Two men in dark suits opened the rear door with military precision. Keith was ushered out, luggage in tow, as though he'd just checked into the world's least inviting Airbnb.

"Not the front door, then?" he muttered under his breath, eyeing the towering façade. "Figures."

Instead, he was herded through a back entrance — a narrow service corridor smelling faintly of damp stone, cabbage, and polish. His suitcase was dragged along behind, bumping indignantly against each stair like a sulky child. After several creaking flights, the men stopped before a heavy wooden door and shoved him through. The hinges shrieked their disapproval.

The attic was dim, moonlight slicing in through dusty windows. Shadows clung to the rafters, the air thick with old timber and the faint smell of mothballs. Not exactly the warmest welcome.

Keith staggered forward, caught his balance, then froze. His eyes adjusted, and there he was — Ryan.

"Ryan?" Keith blurted. "What the hell are you doing here? I tried calling, but your phone's been off."

Ryan, slumped against the wall like a man who'd just failed the world's easiest pub quiz, let out a dry, bitter laugh. "Oh, brilliant. That's rich. Thanks to you, I'm here. They thought I was you—bag over the head, tossed into a van, the whole bloody package. I've had spa treatments more relaxing than that."

Keith winced. "Right. Sorry about that, how was I to know?"

His gaze shifted, and there she was. Melicia. Rising slowly from the chair in the corner, moonlight traces the outline of her face. She stepped forward, quiet but deliberate, eyes fixed on him.

"This is my fault," she said softly, voice shaking despite her best efforts. "Both of you are here because of me."

Keith stared at her, torn somewhere between exasperation and disbelief. She still looked heartbreakingly beautiful—just as she had the last time he'd seen her days ago—only now a little ragged around the edges, hair mussed, eyes weary. His heart softened at the sight, even as his temper bristled. He was upset, grumpy, and more than a little rattled at being dragged into this circus.

"Well… that's nice to hear said out loud finally," he muttered. "Saves me having to piece it together like a crossword puzzle."

Melicia swallowed, her expression carefully unreadable.

Keith's sigh was heavy, but when he spoke, his tone had gentled. "Look, I'm just glad you're both still breathing. But for heaven's sake, Melicia—for the love of tea and sanity—what on earth is this all about?"

The attic seemed to pause, shadows hanging thick as if the room itself were holding its breath. Then Ryan broke the silence, muttering into the gloom:

"If anyone says vampires, I'm out."

Both Keith and Melica stared at him.

Chapter 7

Stringed Attached

Ryan sat slouched in a battered armchair, his fingers drumming a nervous rhythm against his thigh. He had just muttered, half to himself, "Looks like I'm going to die young," and the words still lingered in the air like cigar smoke.

Keith's eyes flicked toward him, then settled on Melicia. She hadn't reacted to Ryan's doom-laden theatrics. Instead, her gaze was fixed on the flames, as though she could find her past smouldering inside the fire. Her lips pressed tight, a thousand words caught behind them.

"Melicia," Keith said softly, not quite a command but close enough. "I'm all ears."

She turned her head. The firelight sharpened the lines of her cheekbones, lending her an almost regal poise—but Keith caught it: the flicker of dread in her eyes.

Ryan leaned forward despite himself, smirking. "This should be good."

Melicia ignored Ryan entirely, her gaze slipping further away, drawn deep into memory. Then, softly but firmly, she spoke. "Do you remember the first time I bumped into you, Keith?"

Keith frowned, leaning forward. "Course I do. We only spoke about it the other day, didn't we?"

Her lips curved faintly, though her eyes stayed sombre. "It wasn't an accident. I did it on purpose."

Ryan gave a low whistle and leaned back in his chair. "Oh, this just keeps getting better and better. Next thing we'll find out, you were secretly the Queen's pastry chef."

"Shut up, Ryan," Keith snapped, eyes fixed on Melicia. "Go on."

Melicia's voice softened, the firelight flickering across her face, as though the flames themselves were dragging the room backwards into her story. "I remember it so clearly—a quiet Sunday evening in Hamburg. I saw you wandering the lanes on your own—hands shoved in your pockets, head full of thoughts. You looked so… ordinary. Safe. Exactly what I needed."

Ryan butted in, grinning. "And so, naturally, you hurled yourself into him like a rugby tackle and snogged him senseless in the street. Romantic, isn't it?"

Keith shot him a glare sharp enough to cut glass. "If you can't shut your mouth, Ryan, at least shut your ears."

Melicia almost smiled at that before continuing. "I nearly sent you stumbling. You didn't know what hit you. I grabbed your arm, held on—and before you could breathe, I kissed you. No hesitation. No permission. I just did it."

Keith rubbed the back of his neck, embarrassed at the memory. "Well, I froze, didn't I? Time just… stopped. A woman like you—magnetic, fearless, impossibly beautiful—was kissing me in the middle of a Hamburg street. My heart was battering my ribs like a drum. I could barely think."

"I noticed two men rush past us," Keith added after a pause, "but I thought it was a coincidence."

"They weren't," Melicia said quietly. "They were Van's men. They'd been after me for days."

Ryan's eyebrows shot up. "So, the great romantic kiss was just a decoy? Brilliant. Poor Keith, thinking it was destiny, when really it was pest control."

"Ryan!" Keith snapped. But the colour rising in his cheeks betrayed him.

Melicia's eyes softened, her voice almost playful. "And then I slipped away, melted into the crowd. Left you standing there, dazed, cheeks bright pink, gawping like you'd just been kissed by an alien. You tried so hard to act casual, but I saw you—glancing around, pretending nothing had happened, while a couple of teenagers giggled at you. You scurried off as a schoolboy caught holding hands behind the bike sheds."

Keith groaned and buried his face in his hands. "Brilliant. My most humiliating moment, and you've been replaying it like a comedy rerun."

Ryan cackled. "Oh, this is gold. Keith, the street Romeo with all the charm of a startled badger."

"Thank you, Ryan," Keith muttered through his fingers. "That really helps."

Melicia ignored him, leaning forward. "But you came back. Three days in a row, to the same street. Waiting. Hoping."

Keith dropped his hands, cheeks burning. "Well… yes."

Melicia's voice grew softer, the memory dragging her backwards. "And then it happened. I slipped behind you, slid my hand into yours, and walked as though I'd always been there. But Van's men were still on my tail. I pulled you into a café, ordered coffee, and pretended everything was normal. And you—" she smiled faintly "—you made me laugh. We clicked."

Keith's voice was quiet now. "I thought it was fate."

"I thought it was survival," she said. "But you were kind. Gentle. When you said you were going back to London, I thought—why not? Why not run with you? Leave everything behind. And for a while… it felt like a new life."

Her voice faltered. "But Van's men found me in London, too. That's when I knew—I couldn't risk you. I had to disappear. So, I faked my death."

Keith's eyes hardened. "You could've told me. I could've helped."

Melicia shook her head slowly. "You don't understand, Keith. Van doesn't stop. He'd have gone through you to get to me. I couldn't let that happen."

She took a deep breath. "You have no idea who Van Jeans really is. He's ruthless, Keith. The kind of man who destroys anyone who crosses him."

Keith frowned. "Then tell me—how did you even get entangled with someone like him?"

Melicia gave a faint, bitter smile. "I met him at an auction. If you want to con a rich fool, you have to blend in with the rich. And what better place than an art auction?"

Ryan, sitting at the edge of the room, grinned. "Well, now I know where I should start looking for my future wife. A rich one."

Melicia shot him a cold look. "This isn't a joke." Then she turned back to Keith. "After the auction, they hosted a wine and dine session for the guests. I noticed Van heading toward the men's washroom. So, I waited. When he came out, I made my move—pretended to rush into the wrong door and bumped into him."

A faint smirk touched her lips. "He helped me up immediately. 'Excuse me, hope you're alright,' he said. I didn't answer. He took my hand and led me to a nearby table. Then I teased him, 'So, do you do this to all the women you bump into?' He smiled but didn't reply. A few seconds later, one of his men whispered something in his ear, and he excused himself. 'Urgent matter,' he said. I thought I had him… but not yet."

Keith leaned forward. "And then?"

"Two days later," Melicia continued, "I was having lunch with a friend when Van appeared again. This time, he approached me directly. He shook my hand and said, 'Hi, how are you?' I smiled back and introduced my friend. He left soon after, but I could feel his eyes on me the whole time."

Ryan couldn't help himself. "Another rich guy to con, huh?"

"Ryan," Keith snapped. "Shut up."

Melicia ignored him. "After lunch, I walked to the car park—and there he was. Van. Waiting beside his car. He told me to get in. It wasn't a request; it was a command. I hesitated… then obeyed."

Her eyes grew distant. "That was the start of it all. Van was charming and patient. Dangerous, but magnetic. Every time we met, I played the part of the elusive woman, and he took the bait. Eventually, he proposed. The wedding was small—held at his mansion. Only a handful of guests, though I'm certain most were his business partners… or criminals."

Keith crossed his arms. "So, what went wrong?"

Melicia's lips curled into a sharp smile. "Nothing went wrong. Everything went exactly as I planned. Midway through the ceremony, his men brought news that one of his illegal dens had been raided by the police. Van left immediately. That was my moment. I went straight into his private study—and there it was, the family heirloom, hanging on the wall like a worthless decoration. I took it… and everything else I could grab."

Ryan raised his eyebrows. "Convenient timing for a police raid during your wedding, huh?"

Melicia looked him dead in the eye. "I was the one who tipped them off. That raid was part of my plan."

Keith's voice softened, almost hesitant. "So that was the last time you saw him?"

Melicia's eyes darkened. "Yes. And knowing Van… I knew I had to get out of the country." She ran a trembling hand through her hair, as if reliving the fear. "I kept a low profile, moved from city to city, never stayed too long in one place. But somehow, he caught up with me."

She gave a bitter laugh. "And there I was—married to you, thinking I'd finally escaped it all. But I hadn't. I could feel his shadow everywhere. His men were watching. Every step I took, every stranger who smiled too long—it felt like him."

Keith clenched his jaw. "You could've told me, Melicia. We could've faced him together."

Melicia shook her head, eyes glistening. "No, Keith. You don't understand. Van doesn't face people—he destroys them. If he found out about you, he'd have gone through you to get to me. I couldn't let that happen."

Her voice broke as she whispered, “So I did the only thing I could—I disappeared. I had to make you believe I was gone… even if it killed me inside.”

Keith’s jaw tightened. It all sounded like something out of a movie. “Then whose body was it in the car?” he asked, his voice low but sharp. “The DNA matched yours.”

Melicia gave a short, bitter laugh. “I had help. My ex-husband—he’s a surgeon. I left him years ago, but the poor fool still adored me. He found a body, altered the records, and planted my DNA.”

Ryan blinked, his eyebrows shooting up. “Hold on. You conned your ex-husband into supplying you with a corpse? That’s… twisted genius, that is.”

Keith’s mouth fell open. “Wait—ex-husband? You were married before Van?”

Melicia gave him a wicked grin. “He wasn’t supposed to be a husband, just a fling. But he proposed, and I thought, why not? He was a surgeon, after all. We got married, went on honeymoon, and that’s where I conned him out of his money and gave him a slip. Poor soul still wants me back.”

Keith nearly choked. “Good God.” He steadied himself and asked, voice trembling, “How many men, Melicia? Before me?”

“Don’t ask her that!” Ryan cut in, waving his hands. “For your sanity, mate, don’t. This will rock you harder than tax season.”

But Melicia ignored him, her eyes fixed on Keith.

“Three,” she said at last. “I was married three times. Van was the third. None of them meant a thing—it was just one con after another. But you…” Her voice softened, eyes glistening in the firelight, “You were different.

You were the one I actually fell in love with. You're the reason I wanted out."

Keith gave a shaky little laugh, somewhere between relief and disbelief. "So, I wasn't dumped, then? You faked your death because of Van? Well—that's rather a relief."

Ryan let out a derisive snort. "Relief? Don't flatter yourself. You were dumped, mate. Fourth husband in the queue, whether you like it or not. Just admit it, pen a tragic ballad, and be done with it."

Melicia turned her head sharply, glaring at him. "You're utterly insufferable, Ryan."

Keith sat in silence, eyes fixed on the floor, his thoughts knotted and raw. Ryan's words stung—because, damn him, there was a flicker of truth hidden in the sarcasm.

The room had fallen into a heavy hush, broken only by the low drone of the air-con. Keith slumped in the armchair, hands clasped tight, staring at the carpet as though it might cough up the answers he'd been chasing for years.

Across the room, Ryan sprawled on the sofa with one leg dangling lazily over the armrest, looking like he hadn't a care in the world. He flicked imaginary dust from his shirt, a smirk tugging at his lips.

At length, he broke the silence. "So, Melicia," he drawled, eyes glinting with curiosity, "how exactly did you pull off that little accident of yours?"

Melicia's gaze shifted between the two men. Keith leaned forward in his chair, jaw clenched tight, the flicker of betrayal still shadowing his face. Ryan, meanwhile, looked amused—like a kid watching a magician about to reveal her trick.

"Well," she began, exhaling slowly, "I hired a car. Simple as that. The manager at the rental agency was... cooperative. He approached me the moment I walked in—all smiles and charm. Poor man probably thought he was in love."

Ryan chuckled. "You really can flirt your way out of anything, can't you?"

Melicia shot him a cool glance. "Flirting is a tool, Ryan. Same as a lockpick or a forged passport. Use it right, it opens doors."

Keith said nothing. He just stared at her, unreadable.

"I made sure the car was booked under my name," she continued. "Let the cameras record me collecting it, signing the papers, even driving off. Everything had to look real. Routine. Traceable. The police love a clean trail—they follow it like dogs to a bone."

Ryan tilted his head. "Ah, breadcrumbs. Hansel and Gretel style. Except your crumbs were made of bureaucracy and CCTV footage. Very British of you."

Melicia ignored him and went on, her tone growing darker. "Then, I drove to a narrow curve off the main road—one with a rusted guardrail and a bad reputation. I saw a car behind me, an older man at the wheel. Perfect witness. Close enough to see what was coming, far enough not to question it."

She paused, eyes distant now, replaying the scene in her mind. "I swerved hard into the pole. Flames, smoke, chaos. A body with my DNA inside—courtesy of my surgeon ex-husband—took care of the rest."

Ryan let out a low whistle, shaking his head in admiration. "That's diabolical. Shakespearean, even. Faked death, grieving lover, perfectly timed witness… If you'd thrown in a poisoned chalice, I'd call it a full play."

Melicia smirked faintly. "I prefer real drama. Less applause, more survival."

Keith finally lifted his gaze. His voice cracked as he asked, "But why? Why go to such extremes, Melicia? Do you know what it did to me—what it still does?"

Her expression softened, and for the first time, her confident façade wavered. "Because, Keith, I wanted you not to think I'd abandoned you. I couldn't bear the thought of you regretting falling in love with me. And I wanted Van to leave us alone, once and for all."

Keith shook his head, eyes glistening. "You made me believe you were gone. Do you know how many nights I—" His voice faltered, swallowed by the weight of grief that still lingered.

Melicia moved closer, placing a hand gently on his arm. "I've handled similar situations before. You weren't meant to carry all that pain forever. I needed you safe."

Ryan coughed theatrically. "Touching and really touching. But just so you know, if you'd told me sooner, I could've saved you the trouble. I've faked being dead many times—usually at work to avoid meetings."

Despite himself, Keith let out a faint chuckle, though his eyes never left Melicia's.

Ryan leaned back with a grin. "There we go. A laugh. That's my good deed done for the day."

Melicia smiled faintly, but her hand remained on Keith's, steady and firm.

Melicia's lips tightened into a small smile. "I wanted you to cash in the insurance money, Keith. To be free. To live without worrying about me, I know you needed that."

"I didn't cash it," Keith said firmly, shaking his head. "You know why? Because I knew you were alive. The tattoo gave it away."

"What tattoo?" Melicia asked, her curiosity piqued.

"The body I saw at the morgue had a tattoo on the left shoulder. Yours is on your hip," Keith replied sharply.

"Ohhh! I see… clever of you. Perks of seeing me naked," Melicia said, her tone laced with seduction as she tried to divert Keith from the subject.

"Thanks to me," Ryan cut in smugly, puffing out his chest. "I was the one who spotted you on Instagram and told Keith you were alive. Honestly, Melicia, you've only got yourself to blame for being so damn photogenic."

Melicia shot him a daggered look. "And thanks to you, Van's men found me again. Even Glasgow wasn't safe."

Silence fell. The fire hissed and cracked, the shadows shifting. The weight of Melicia's past—her cons, her lies, her survival—thickened the air until it was almost suffocating.

"Now, if you two are finished with the melodrama," Ryan grumbled, folding his arms like a sulky child who'd been forced to watch a soap opera, "can you maybe—oh, I don't know—figure out how to get us out of here?"

Keith shot Ryan a glare sharp enough to cut glass, but Melicia straightened, her tone steady and commanding. "I know what Van wants," she said, eyes moving between the two men. "We'll get it for him. But not tonight. Tonight, we rest. Tomorrow… tomorrow will be big."

Ryan snorted, throwing his arms up dramatically. "Rest? In this palace? Five stars at best. I'll be sure to leave a glowing review on Yelp—assuming we're not six feet under by sunrise." He dragged a rickety chair across the cracked tiles and flopped into it, brushing dust off like royalty. "Behold, my royal throne," he muttered, stretching out and wincing when the chair creaked dangerously.

Keith, unimpressed, turned his attention back to Melicia. They both eyed the filthy mattress shoved in the corner. It smelled of damp, rust, and broken promises—but Keith said nothing. Instead, he reached out and found her hand. She didn't hesitate; her fingers curled around his, thumb stroking across his knuckles in a wordless reassurance.

"Don't worry," Melicia whispered, her voice softer than the silence pressing in around them. "I've handled worse situations. We will get through this one."

Keith leaned in and kissed her. It wasn't rushed, not desperate—just honest. She returned it, her lips firm, steady, before turning in his arms and settling against him, her back fitting into the curve of his chest. She pulled his hand to her waist, and he held her there, the warmth between them fighting off the cold concrete and filthy mattress.

His chest tightened. He'd never admit aloud how much that comfort meant. From the other side of the room came Ryan's muffled groan. "Oh, brilliant. Lovers' retreat in an abandoned warehouse. Does anyone want to book me a different room? Maybe with a mint on the pillow? No? Fine. But if you two start snoring in harmony, I'm walking out."

Melicia chuckled softly against Keith's arm. Keith only shook his head, pressing his face into her hair.

The night settled into fragile quiet—three hearts bracing, in their own ways, for the storm that tomorrow would unleash.

Chapter 8

Ten Million Reasons To Complain

Suddenly, the heavy oak door burst open with a bang that rattled the cutlery on the dining table downstairs. Ryan nearly fell off the chair he'd been dozing in, his arms flailing like a startled chicken. Keith and Melicia jolted awake on the filthy mattress, blinking in the half-light.

"Up. Now," barked one of Van's men, gesturing sharply with his rifle. Two others waited at the doorway, eyes like hawks.

Ryan muttered under his breath, tugging at his crumpled shirt as he stood. "Well, looks like this is it. End of the road, lads. We had a good run."

"Stop your whining," Melicia hissed, brushing her tangled hair back with a snap of her wrist.

Keith shuffled between them like a man trapped in a very awkward lift, muttering, "Please—for once—could we just walk in silence?"

The trio was herded down the broad staircase, flanked by Van's men in front and behind. The marble floors gleamed under the morning light, making the whole place feel more like a museum than a home.

At the far end of the cavernous dining room sat Van himself, leisurely enjoying his breakfast. He dabbed his mouth with a linen napkin, as if the armed escorts and the three unwilling guests were nothing more than an interruption in his morning routine.

"Ah, here you are," he said smoothly, lifting his glass of orange juice in mock salute. "I started without you. My deepest apologies. Please—join me. I'm sure you're hungry. Especially you, my love." His eyes lingered on Melicia.

They sat at the long mahogany table, plates quietly filled by Van's maidservants. No one spoke. Only the clink of cutlery and the faint crackle of the fire broke the silence.

"You've not been to this mansion before, have you, Melicia?" Van said at last, slicing through his eggs with surgical neatness. "Shame. You could've had all of this. We might have been wonderful together—you, wrapped in luxury, me by your side. But instead, you chose betrayal."

Melicia's fork pressed into her plate with a sharp clink. "Let's not dress it up, Van. Get to the point."

His eyes glittered, taking pleasure in her defiance. "Very well. You know what I want. You have forty-eight hours to get it. And…" He dabbed his lips with a napkin. "And you will pay me ten million dollars for the trouble you caused."

Melicia's chair scraped as she leaned forward, clutching her butter knife as if it might suddenly turn into a real blade. "That's low—even for you.

You already have everything. Another ten million isn't going to make you richer!"

Van's smile was slow, deliberate. "That," he said smoothly, "is the price you pay."

Keith froze with toast halfway to his mouth, his eyes darting nervously between them. Ryan, meanwhile, let his fork clatter dramatically onto his plate.

"Oh, brilliant," Ryan muttered. "Extortion with a side of sausages. I'm loving this."

Melicia ignored him, her gaze locked on Van. "Forty-eight hours isn't enough. You want results, you give me more time."

Van's smile thinned. "Time is expensive. Perhaps I should hold one of your companions as collateral. The loud one, perhaps." He gestured lazily toward Ryan, who nearly choked on his own spit.

"Me?" Ryan's voice cracked. "Oh, no, no, no—you've got the wrong bloke. I don't even know them properly! I was dragged into this circus. I've got a dentist appointment next week, for crying out loud. You don't want me!"

Van smirked. "On the contrary, you'll do nicely."

Ryan buried his face in his hands. "Unbelievable. I'm about to become ravenous with gingivitis."

Melicia's voice cut through his whining, steady and hard. "No. You don't take either of them. I need both if I'm going to pull this off."

Van arched a brow. "Why?"

"Because," she snapped, "I didn't lose your heirloom on purpose. Star Pawn in Glasgow conned me. They cheated me, flipped it, and it's already changed hands. To find it, I'll need Keith's contacts and..." She flicked her eyes at Ryan. "His particular... talents."

"Talents?" Ryan squeaked. "Since when do I have talents?"

Keith cleared his throat, his voice low. "You do talk an awful lot. Maybe that counts."

"Fantastic," Ryan muttered. "So, I'm the chatterbox mascot in this suicide mission."

Melicia leaned closer across the table, her eyes sharp as blades on Van. "You want your twenty–million–dollar trinket back?" she said, her voice low, laced with venom. "Then you'll let me keep both of them. Take one, and you sabotage yourself. I'm not bluffing."

The room froze. Even the clink of cutlery halted. Van's knife hovered mid-slice before he slowly set it down. He leaned back in his chair, studying her as though she were some rare, dangerous animal.

"You've grown bold, Melicia," he murmured, his tone smooth yet edged. "I almost admire it."

His hand twitched—a subtle gesture—and one of his men dragged a bound and gagged figure into the light, tossing him at Melicia's feet like a discarded parcel. The man's muffled groans filled the silence.

Ryan stiffened. Keith leaned in closer to Melicia, his whisper sharp against her ear. "Who the hell is this?"

Melicia's lips curled. "He's the one who stole from me. The one who thought he could cheat me."

Van's smile widened, a predator's grin. "Melicia, meet Mr Digger. I believe you two are already acquainted. Turns out your story checks out. We decided to take the liberty of fetching him here... save you the trouble."

Keith exchanged a glance with Ryan, both men floored by the turn of events.

"Digger!" Melicia snapped, her voice like a whip. "Serves you right for stealing from me—and for thinking you could get away with it. Now, tell us who you sold it to."

Van's men tore the gag from Digger's mouth. He coughed, shaking, eyes darting between Melicia and Van.

"I… I'm sorry, Mr Van," he stammered. "Had I known it belonged to you, I'd never have dared pawn it."

Van's gaze hardened, cold enough to freeze the room. His voice was low but unyielding. "Spare me your apologies. Answer the question—who did you pawn it to?"

Digger's Adam's apple bobbed as he swallowed, his voice breaking. "I-It was… Dr. Sevins. A known Oncologist."

Van tilted his head, studying him with quiet disdain. "How much?"

"Ten million dollars," Digger stammered. His hands shook as if the number itself might draw blood.

Van's eyes narrowed, his tone calm but laced with steel. "My twenty-million-dollar family heirloom… sold for half its worth?"

Digger jerked back, a sharp flinch running through him as his voice split with panic. "I didn't know, Mr Van! I swear! If I'd known it was yours, I wouldn't have laid a finger on it!" The words tumbled out in a frantic rush—part excuse, part desperate plea—before dying off into a miserable hush. He shrank into himself, doing his best to look remorseful under Van's unblinking stare.

Van let the silence stretch until it was unbearable. Then, with a slight shift of his eyes, he turned back to Melicia. His voice was almost conversational, but every word carried weight. "There you go. I've made your life easy. Get it back—and bring me ten million more—within forty-eight hours."

The words dropped like chains on the table.

Van's gaze flicked to the trembling pawnshop owner sprawled on the floor. "And as for Mr Digger…" He smiled faintly, a predator's smile. "He's our guest until then. Consider it collateral."

Melicia's jaw tightened, her eyes steady, but her fingers dug into the table's edge until her knuckles whitened. She didn't argue—she knew she had no ground to stand on, not with Keith and Ryan sitting under Van's shadow.

Van leaned forward, his voice dropping to a velvet whisper, laced with poison. "We'll be watching you. All three of you. Don't mistake this for mercy. You won't get a second chance."

The silence that followed was suffocating, heavy with unspoken fear.

Ryan's knuckles whitened against his glass. Keith shifted uneasily, eyes darting between Melicia and Van, calculating every possible outcome.

Melicia met Van's stare without flinching, then gave the faintest nod—her mind already racing, the weight of the stakes pressing harder than ever. Pushing back her chair, she rose and headed for the door.

Keith noticed immediately, abandoning his half-eaten breakfast to follow her without question.

Ryan, however, stayed planted in his seat, still chewing. Only when he realised the other two were already halfway to the door did he scramble up. "Oi! Hold on for me!" he called, waving his fork. "At least let me finish this. It's bad manners to leave the table like that, you know."

The heavy oak doors of Van's mansion shut behind them with a boom that reverberated through the corridor. Two of his men shadowed their every step, silent but suffocating in their presence.

Keith shoved his hands into his pockets, muttering just loud enough for Melicia to hear. "Well, that went marvellously. A casual breakfast, a bit of light extortion, and now forty-eight hours to pull off the impossible. Splendid."

Ryan nearly tripped on the carpet runner, his voice cracking. "I told you—I'm not even supposed to be here! What is this, Melicia? Van thinks you owe him ten million and some priceless trinket? Since when are you running with art thieves?!"

Melicia stopped abruptly, forcing both men to stumble into her. She turned, eyes like sharpened glass. "You think I like being paraded around like a bargaining chip? That I chose this mess?"

Keith lifted his hands in mock surrender, though his voice carried a bite. "Forgive me, darling, but from where I'm standing, you seem awfully cosy at the high-stakes table. The rest of us are just collateral."

Ryan jabbed a finger at her. "Collateral? I am collateral! They're keeping that Digger bloke, but did you hear Van? 'We'll keep a close watch on you three.' That means me too! I don't even like tea parties with gangsters!"

Melicia exhaled sharply, the fire in her eyes giving way to something steadier, colder. She leaned closer to both men, lowering her voice so the guards would miss more than whispers. "Listen to me, both of you. I can't do this without you. Van doesn't believe it, but I know it's true. That trinket—they call it twenty million, but it's worth more than that. And the man who holds it now? Dr Sevins? He won't give it up easily. Which means…"

She paused, letting her words sink in.

"…you two had better decide quickly if you're in this with me. Because if you're not, you won't live long enough to complain about it."

Keith blinked at her, the gruff mask slipping just enough to show unease. Ryan stared like he'd just been sentenced to death.

The guards gestured impatiently for them to move along. The trio walked on, the silence thicker than before—but charged with unspoken decisions and a dangerous, fragile alliance.

The trio pressed forward, silence weighing heavily between them, thick with unspoken doubts and the fragile thread of an uneasy alliance. "What we need is a proper bath," Ryan muttered.

"I know just the place," Melicia replied. Outside Van's mansion, they stuck out their thumbs for a lift—and, at last, one came.

The pig truck rattled along the dirt road, every bump sending Ryan and Keith lurching into the squealing livestock. The stench was overwhelming. Ryan clutched the wooden slats of the truck bed like his life depended on it.

"This," he gagged, "is how I die. Crushed between bacon and bad decisions."

Keith wiped something unpleasant off his sleeve, glaring at Melicia's silhouette up front in the cab. "Of course she gets the clean seat," he muttered. "And of course we get tetanus."

By the time they reached the city, both men looked like they had just crawled out of a barn fire. When the driver pulled over, Melicia thanked the older man with a sweet smile and a quick peck on the cheek before striding away without a single glance back.

They stumbled after her, through narrow streets, until she stopped in front of a sleek, glass-walled tower. One swipe of her palm against a biometric scanner, and the doors whispered open.

Ryan froze, blinking. “Uh… Melicia? You’ve got… James Bond villain real estate? Since when?”

Keith’s eyes darted to the hidden cameras tucked in corners. “Biometric locks, retina scanners… is this an apartment or NASA headquarters?”

“More like a safehouse,” crackled Ryan.

Melicia ignored them, gliding ahead. Inside, the apartment stretched out like something from a luxury magazine—chrome fixtures, floor-to-ceiling windows, a panoramic city view.

Ryan whistled low. “Yeah, okay. I’m officially convinced you dated an arms dealer. Or a football team.”

Melicia didn’t respond. Instead, she dropped her coat, kicked off her heels, and disappeared straight into the master bath without a word. The sound of running water followed.

Ryan scratched his head, then spotted another bathroom. “Right. If we’re playing pretend criminals, at least I’ll smell like a clean one.” He vanished inside.

Keith wandered deeper, eventually opening the door to a sprawling bedroom with its own marble bath. His jaw dropped. “Unbelievable. A football team could live in here and still have room for their cheerleaders.”

He ran a hand across the polished counter, muttering to himself. “And here I thought we were hiding out in some dingy motel. Should’ve known she had a penthouse tucked away.”

From somewhere down the hall, Ryan's muffled voice echoed out of the bathroom. "Call me paranoid, but doesn't anyone else wonder why she really has this place?!"

Keith shook his head, sinking onto the edge of the massive bed. "Paranoid? I'd call it a survival instinct. Trouble is, she's steering this ship, and we're just along for the sinking."

The sound of Melicia's shower cut off. A few seconds later, her voice carried through the apartment—sharp, commanding, with no room for protest.

"Both of you—living room. Now. We don't have time for your jokes."

Ryan muttered, "There goes our bubble bath."

Keith groaned, "There goes our lives."

But they obeyed, padding nervously toward whatever storm Melicia was about to unleash.

They filed into the living room, the city's skyline glittering through the glass walls like a thousand watchful eyes. Melicia was already waiting, hair damp, wrapped in a robe that looked far too elegant to be improvised. She stood with her arms folded, the very picture of composure—until you noticed the steel in her eyes.

Keith and Ryan dropped onto the couch like schoolboys summoned to the headmistress's office.

Melicia didn't sit. She paced. "Van's given us forty-eight hours. Forty-eight. That's barely enough time to breathe, let alone track down an heirloom pawned to a surgeon with too much money and not enough conscience."

Ryan threw his hands up. "Excuse me, backtrack a little—an Oncologist? As in scalpels, stitches, and bedside manner? Why on earth does a doctor need a twenty-million-dollar trinket?!"

"Because," Melicia shot back, "collectors don't always collect stamps. Some want power, while others seek leverage. Dr Sevins? He wants both."

Keith leaned forward, elbows on his knees. "Alright. So, we knock on his door, ask politely, and he hands it over? Or do we—" He gestured vaguely. "—break in and play jewel thieves?"

Melicia finally stopped pacing, fixing him with a look that made him regret opening his mouth. "We don't ask. And we don't 'play' anything. We get it back. Quietly. Efficiently. Without Van's men breathing down our necks. Because believe me—if we fail, they won't just kill me. They'll kill you, too."

Ryan paled, tugging at his shirt collar like it was strangling him. "Wonderful. Fantastic. Forty-eight hours to steal from a maniac doctor while being babysat by gangsters. Just out of curiosity—what's Plan B?"

"There is no Plan B." Melicia's voice was low, confident. "We succeed, or we disappear."

The words hung in the air, heavy as chains.

Ryan sank back into the couch with a groan. "Disappearing sounds better by the minute."

Keith glanced at him, then back at Melicia, trying to mask the knot of unease tightening in his chest. He'd followed her this far, but every step seemed to dig them deeper into a pit with no bottom.

And yet… he couldn't ignore the fire in her eyes.

"Alright," he said finally. "Where do we start?"

Melicia allowed herself the faintest hint of a smile. “First—we find out who he is and where Dr Sevins keeps his collection. And then… we take it back.”

Ryan dropped his head into his hands. “Of course we do. Why not? Let’s add ‘grand larceny’ to my CV.”

Keith smirked despite himself. “Cheer up. May not be as bad.”

Ryan glared at him. “Bad? BAD?! It’s like from the frying pan into the fire.”

CHAPTER 9

HUSTLING HEARTS

Melicia had had enough of their bickering. She snapped her laptop open, the sharp sound cutting through their chatter. Her fingers moved across the keys with practised precision, her face set in a focused expression.

Keith leaned back in his chair with a smirk. “I can help.”

Ryan snorted, clutching his drink like a lifeline. “Let’s see what she comes up with.”

Melicia ignored them both, her screen filling with images of Dr Sevins—tailored suits, a chiselled jawline, and that smug, too-polished smile.

“He’s not just a plastic surgeon,” she said flatly.

Keith craned his neck. “Looks like one to me. Probably charges ten grand to remove a wrinkle.”

"Shut up for once," she snapped, eyes never leaving the screen. "This man rebuilds faces. Identities. Criminals, politicians, celebrities… anyone rich enough to buy a new life."

Ryan nearly choked on his drink. "So, he's, like… a witness protection program with knives?"

"More like a puppeteer," Melicia said, scrolling deeper. "And his puppets pay to vanish."

The article she pulled up painted a picture of exclusivity: an iron-gated clinic, a tight three-day schedule, and whispers of private consultations—the fortress of a man who thrived in shadows.

Then she slowed. Post after post showed Sevins with women—always the same kind. Tall. Blonde. Impeccable.

Melicia narrowed her eyes. "There it is."

Keith leaned forward, curious. "What, his secret stash of botched jobs?"

"No." She tilted the screen just enough for them to see. "This. His weakness. Ego. Validation. Women like that are his soft spot."

Ryan raised a brow. "So… what, we get a blonde wig and hope for the best?"

"A gambling addict too, I see," Melicia muttered under her breath, clicking through a few more pages. "Always at the casino… He's got a taste for risk, doesn't he?"

It made sense. His penchant for beautiful women, as well as the thrill of tennis matches and high-stakes gambling, spoke of someone with an insatiable need for excitement. A man who craved power and luxury, yet was easily swayed by the right offer—a man who would make mistakes when caught in a web of indulgence.

She turned back to the couch, where Ryan and Keith were lounging, utterly uninterested in her findings. Ryan was fiddling with his phone, clearly waiting for the next moment of action, while Keith half-heartedly flipped through a magazine. Neither of them had anything worthwhile to contribute at the moment.

"I know how we can get hold of Dr Sevins," she said, her voice cutting through the idle chatter. They both looked up, startled by the sudden shift in her tone.

Ryan blinked. "Oh, do you now? Please, enlighten us."

Melicia shot him a glance, her lips curling into a slight, knowing smile. "His weakness is his vanity. His obsession is with women, status, and feeling important. But it's not just that. I've seen his patterns. He plays tennis to socialise, and spends far too much time gambling at casinos. He likes the thrill, the risk, the games. He's unpredictable, and that's exactly what we need to exploit."

Keith frowned, still processing the information. "So, we just stroll into a casino, what, and get him to hand over the heirloom?"

"Not quite," Melicia said, shaking her head with a small, knowing smile. "Every evening, he plays tennis at a prestigious Rotary club where only members are allowed."

"How are we supposed to get in?" Ryan asked, scepticism lacing his voice.

Melicia shrugged. "I don't know yet, but we'll figure it out when we're there."

Keith shook his head, looking defeated. "I don't even know how to play tennis..."

Ryan shot him a teasing grin, leaning back in his seat. "All you have to do is hold a racket and hit the ball, mate. It's not rocket science."

Keith ran a hand through his hair, growing increasingly frustrated. "But we don't even have tennis rackets or proper sportswear..."

The two of them started arguing, their voices rising as they bantered back and forth, both getting more worked up. Melicia watched them for a moment, arms crossed and a smirk tugging at the corners of her lips. It was like watching two children squabble, utterly oblivious to the urgency of the situation.

With a sigh, she pushed herself off the couch, her heels clicking sharply against the floor as she walked away. "Enough," she said, cutting through their squabble with a commanding tone. "I'm going to get ready. You two figure it out."

She disappeared into the bedroom, leaving the two men to argue further. The sound of their voices drifted faintly from behind the door, but Melicia was focused. She needed to look the part—she needed to be flawless if she was going to pull this off. She chose a dress that was sleek and elegant, hugging her curves perfectly. When she stepped out of the bedroom, the transformation was immediate.

Keith and Ryan both froze, their mouths agape as they looked her up and down. Her dress was stunning, a deep shade of crimson that shimmered under the soft light of the apartment. Her hair cascaded down her shoulders in soft waves, and her makeup was flawless. She exuded confidence and power.

"Well, what do you think?" Melicia asked, hands on her hips, with a sly smile. "Think I'll get a lift into the Rotary Club now?"

Keith, still trying to collect himself, managed to stammer, "You... You look like a million-dollar doll."

Ryan, with a raised eyebrow and a wicked grin, quipped, "Ha, more like a con woman."

Keith scoffed, but before he could respond, he and Ryan started playfully bickering, a mixture of competitive energy and frustration. Keith lunged at Ryan, sending them both tumbling onto the couch as they wrestled each other. They were back to being like children again, completely distracted by their own antics.

Melicia stood there, watching the spectacle with a bemused smile. Finally, she snapped, "Enough!" Her voice was sharp, but there was no real anger in it—just the kind of authority that made it clear she was in charge. "Go and get dressed—something casual. We're going to play tennis."

Ryan looked up, confusion crossing his face. "Tennis? Wait—what?"

"You heard me," Melicia replied, her voice steady and confident. "You may not know how to play, but we're going to get inside that club, and once we do, I'll handle Dr Sevins."

She knew exactly what she was doing. Being a woman who had perfected the art of manipulation and getting what she wanted, Melicia was more than capable of getting into the exclusive Rotary Club. It was all about confidence, allure, and the ability to play the game.

Keith and Ryan finally stood, still grumbling but moving toward their rooms. The next few minutes were a blur of hasty dressing and rushed movements. They were out the door and into the elevator before they knew it. Melicia was already standing beside a sleek black sports car, the engine purring softly under the hood. Her eyes glinted with the thrill of what was to come, and she exuded an air of confidence that made the two men uneasy.

Keith, wide-eyed, was the first to speak. "Is this... your car?"

Ryan raised an eyebrow, his grin growing. "One of her ex-husbands, I presume?"

Melicia rolled her eyes, then slid into the driver's seat with a fluid grace that seemed almost too natural. "It's mine for now," she replied coolly, ignoring their teasing. "Now, get in."

Keith hesitated, but did as he was told, sliding into the passenger seat. Ryan reluctantly climbed into the back, his eyes darting around nervously. The interior of the car smelled faintly of leather and expensive perfume—a stark contrast to the rough, chaotic reality of their situation.

Melicia's fingers gripped the steering wheel, and within seconds, the engine roared to life. She slammed her foot on the accelerator, and the car shot forward like a bullet. The streets blurred as she navigated through traffic with precision, her movements sharp and quick.

Keith's heart raced, his grip tightening on the door. "Melicia—slow down, will you?" he shouted over the roar of the engine.

Ryan, holding on for dear life in the backseat, managed to croak, "Yeah, we're not exactly in a race here!"

But Melicia barely seemed to notice. Her eyes were fixed on the road, her focus unwavering. She drove like a woman who had done this a thousand times, each turn calculated and precise. The speed, the danger—it was almost like she thrived on it.

Keith glanced at her, eyes wide with disbelief. This woman, the one he had married, was a mystery to him. How could someone so composed, so dangerous, have been living a life he never even suspected? He was a part-time teacher, a librarian—he had no idea how he had ended up here, with her, in this world of fast cars, secrets, and danger.

As they sped toward their destination, Keith's mind raced. She's way out of my league, he thought to himself. Why on earth did she even marry a loser like me? What did I have to offer? He tried to push the thought aside, but it lingered. How had he ended up in this whirlwind of deception?

"Keith," Melicia's voice broke through his thoughts, and he looked over to find her watching him, her expression unreadable.

He swallowed hard. "Yeah?"

"You're wondering how you fit into all of this," she said, her voice surprisingly soft. "Just keep your head in the game. We've got one chance at this."

Keith nodded, but his heart was pounding. This was a different world than anything he'd ever known, and with every second that ticked by, it seemed like he was falling further into it.

Melicia's eyes gleamed as she made another sharp turn, the road ahead lighting up with the glow of city lights. The destination was near, and everything was about to change.

Keith wasn't sure whether he was ready for it, but there was no turning back now.

The sleek black sports car screeched to a halt outside the Rotary Club. The guard at the gate barely had time to register the blur of headlights before the engine purred down. Keith and Ryan climbed out stiff-legged, both pale as paper.

"Are you trying to kill us?" Keith muttered, still gripping the door as though for dear life. Ryan leaned against the car, gasping. "If I die, it won't be from Dr Sevins. It'll be from whiplash."

Melicia ignored them. She was busy scanning the arrivals. Mercedes, Jaguars, and Porsches lined the drive. Then—perfect—she spotted him: a bald, stout man in an ill-fitting linen blazer, climbing out of a brand-new Porsche with the proud look of a man who thought money could buy him taste.

"Target acquired," she murmured. Without a second thought, she strutted straight towards him and—"Oh!"—deliberately stumbled into his chest. Her clutch bag tumbled dramatically onto the pavement.

"Oh, heavens, I am so sorry!" Melicia gasped, fluttering her lashes as though the accident had shocked her.

The man steadied her with both hands. "No, no, no trouble at all," he said, his voice thick with self-importance. "Are you hurt, darling?"

From the car, Ryan whispered to Keith, "She just body-checked a Porsche owner. Watch and learn." Keith shook his head, muttering, "I didn't find her… she found me. Remember that."

Meanwhile, Melicia retrieved her clutch and looked up at the man with an apologetic smile. "I'm such a klutz sometimes. New heels, no balance - a terrible combination. You must think me ridiculous."

"Not at all!" He straightened proudly. "Arnold Melville. Banker. And you are…?" "Melicia," she purred, taking his arm before he could think twice. "You must allow me to make it up to you, Mr Melville. At least let me buy you a drink?"

Arnold's chest puffed. "I wouldn't dream of letting a lady pay. Come, the bar's just inside. You'll adore it."

Keith and Ryan exchanged looks as they watched Melicia sail through the club gates on Melville's arm. Ryan whistled. "What a woman." Keith's reply was grim. "She's not my woman, she is my wife."

Inside the Rotary Club's lounge, the air was rich with cigar smoke and money. Men in polos and tennis whites discussed stocks, politics, and mistresses. Arnold ushered Melicia into a plush leather booth and waved for the waiter.

"Martini, darling?" he asked, signalling. "Make it two," she said with a smile.

Arnold leaned closer, his eyes twinkling. "Tell me, what's a stunning lady like you doing here all alone?" "Well…"

Melicia sighed dramatically. "I was supposed to meet a friend. He promised to play a match with me, but—" she shrugged prettily—"he stood me up."

Arnold's face crumpled in mock outrage. "The fool! A woman like you, left waiting? Criminal." He raised his glass. "To a better company." They clinked glasses, Melicia laughing softly as she took a sip.

As Arnold rambled about his golf handicap, Melicia leaned in, lowering her voice. "So, tell me… what's the crowd like here? I mean, it must be full of the city's best people."

Arnold grinned, eager to boast. "The crème de la crème. Judges, surgeons, CEOs… oh, and Sevins."

Melicia tilted her head. "Sevins?" "Yes, Dr Sevins,"

Arnold nodded. "Plastic surgeon to the stars. Plays here most evenings. Gambling problem, too, but a genius with a scalpel. He'll be in tonight, without fail."

As if on cue, the doors opened and in walked Dr Sevins—tall, immaculately dressed, with the polished confidence of a man who knew too many secrets. He spotted Melicia instantly. His eyes lingered, his lips curving into a wolfish smile.

"Melville!" Sevins greeted, striding over. "And who's this enchanting lady you're hiding away?" Arnold chuckled, puffing out his chest. "This, my dear fellow, is—" Before he could finish, Melicia rose gracefully, extending her hand. "Melicia. A pleasure, Doctor. I've heard so much about you."

Sevins kissed her hand, eyes never leaving hers. "All lies, I hope." She smiled slyly. "That depends. Are the lies more interesting than the truth?"

Arnold blinked, looking between them. "Well, I—" But the air between Melicia and Sevins was already charged, a cat-and-mouse electricity.

The conversation between Melicia and Dr Sevins is now in full swing, with the tension subtly rising. Sevins leans in closer, his smile widening as Melicia expertly navigates the conversation.

Melicia catches his gaze, her voice dropping lower in that seductive, almost conspiratorial way. "So, Dr. Sevins... I've heard a few things about your expertise. You're not just a surgeon, are you?"

Sevins' eyebrow lifts slightly; a gleam of curiosity mixed with pride in his expression. "Not just a surgeon, no. I tend to... broaden my horizons." His voice grows more intimate. "What exactly did you hear?"

Melicia smiles cryptically. "Oh, just whispers here and there. You know, a man who can alter appearances might also be able to... create new ones entirely. Isn't that what some people need? A fresh start?"

Sevins chuckles softly, leaning back in his seat as he takes another sip of his drink. "You have an interesting mind, Melicia. But you're right. Some people do seek new identities—if the price is right."

Melicia looks around the club lounge, her eyes flicking to the high-rollers and the plush decor, before returning to him. "I imagine the people who come here—do they ever need, you know, more than just a face change? What about... other things?" She lets the question linger in the air.

Dr Sevins tilts his head, intrigued by her directness. "You're quite bold. But, yes... sometimes a person's reputation needs to change more than their face. Money can buy a lot of things in this world—status, power..." He looks at her, his eyes narrowing slightly, "...protection."

A small smile tugs at Melicia's lips. "Protection, hmm? So, Dr Sevins... tell me, who do you associate with when it comes to... let's call them, high-profile individuals?" She pauses, leaning in a bit closer. "You don't mind sharing, do you?"

Sevins leaned in, his voice lowering, obviously drawn in by Melicia's charm. "I'm sure you're not too interested in the details of my clients, are you?"

Melicia let the words hang in the air, a slow smile creeping up her face. "How intriguing," she murmured, her tone calm and deliberate. "Dr Sevins, do you still make regular visits to your clinic, or do you prefer the peace of places like this?"

He gave a grin that bordered on smug, clearly enjoying the attention. "A man's gotta keep his options open, right? The clinic's still running, though. Steady stream of clients—some wealthy, some... well, they prefer to stay out of the spotlight."

Melicia's gaze sharpened, her curiosity piqued. She had her next question ready, but she let the moment for just a beat longer, watching him squirm slightly in the heavy silence. "Tell me, Dr Sevins, do you have a lot of women like me around? Seems like you have quite the... fondness for them."

He chuckled, tilting his head slightly as he leaned back. "Well, appreciating beauty's hardly a crime. I'm a man of taste. And honestly, what's the harm in that?"

Melicia leaned back, too, but there was a coolness to her now, something calculated. "That's an interesting answer," she mused, as if she were weighing his words. She raised an eyebrow. "How long will you be here, Dr Sevins?"

He glanced at his watch, momentarily distracted by the question. "Just for the evening. A few things to handle before I head back. But the night's still young. If you're up for it, I'm about to head to the back lounge for a game of cards. Care to join me?"

Melicia's smile sharpened—now she had him exactly where she wanted him. "A game of cards, huh? Perhaps after that, you can show me more of what this place has to offer. I always enjoy meeting... interesting people."

As she spoke, her gaze briefly shifted toward the bar, where she noticed Keith and Ryan sitting at a nearby table. They had managed to slip into the club unnoticed. Ryan, clearly out of his element, gripped his drink tightly, his unease palpable in the exclusive atmosphere. Keith, on the other hand, appeared more at ease but kept glancing anxiously toward the door, as if waiting for something to happen.

Melicia stood, her movement graceful and confident. "I'll join you for that game, Dr Sevins," she said, her voice dropping just a little as she leaned in slightly closer. "But after that... we'll see if you can show me the other things this place has to offer."

Without waiting for a response, she turned toward Arnold, leaning in to plant a light kiss on his cheek. "Hope you don't mind me going with Dr Sevins for a bit."

Arnold grinned, unfazed, his voice dripping with playful indifference. “Well, a woman wants what she wants.”

Melicia’s grin widened, then she turned, her hips swaying just enough to leave a trail of undeniable allure as she walked away, every step measured to keep Dr Sevins right on her heels.

Sevins’ eyes followed her, a mix of admiration and desire flashing in them as he stood, ready to follow her like a moth to a flame.

Keith and Ryan exchanged a look, both a little out of their depth but equally impressed. Ryan leaned in, his voice barely a whisper, “Did she just... play him?”

Keith gave a low chuckle, still watching Melicia lead Sevins toward the back lounge. “She didn’t just play him. She’s got him wrapped around her finger.”

Melicia, now seated in the back lounge, was already making herself comfortable. With Dr Sevins beside her, she knew exactly what to do next. The conversation was hers to steer, and she would do it with the same effortless grace she had used to get this far. Every word, every look was a carefully calculated move. And she wasn’t about to break a sweat.

Chapter 10

Loops, Lips, And Lousy Luck

The evening unfolded as planned for Melicia, with Ryan causing a deliberate commotion at the neighbouring table while Keith seethed at the sight of her cosying up to Dr Sevins.

Melicia leaned in, her fingers grazing Sevins's wrist as she purred, "Perhaps we should place a wager of our own, Doctor. But I suspect the stakes you crave go far beyond mere money, don't they?"

Sevins smirked, his eyes gleaming with predatory intrigue. "You're sharp, Melicia. You'd be wasted on these... social charades. Why don't we continue this game somewhere private? My home. A proper match... just you and me."

She tilted her head, feigning a moment's hesitation. "Oh? Do you whisper that line to all the ladies you wine and dine?"

He leaned closer, his tone firm and commanding. "I'm very choosy—I only invite the special ones. Come. You won't regret it. Perhaps I can even examine you... offer some advice on a makeover."

She let her lips curve into the faintest smile, crafting the illusion of yielding. "Are you saying I have flaws?"

"I didn't mean it that way," he chuckled, "but there's always room for a little... enhancement."

"Well… if you insist, I suppose I can give it a try. Let me freshen up," Melicia said. She rose from her seat, letting her fingers trail lightly across his shoulders with deliberate grace. Then she walked off—hips swaying in a slow, confident rhythm. Sevins watched her go, eyes following every curve as she slipped toward the washroom with that effortless catwalk glide.

Inside, the washroom glittered with mirrors and soft lighting, the air thick with perfume and idle conversations. Keith pushed through the door a moment later, and a chorus of reactions rippled through the room—one woman gasped and clutched her handbag, another gave an exaggerated eye-roll. But one woman only smirked, boldly giving him a head-to-toe once-over.

Keith lifted both hands in an apologetic gesture of surrender. "Sorry, ladies. Emergency. Just… pretend I'm invisible, yeah?"

Melicia whirled on him. "I was expecting you sooner."

"You dragged me into this circus—I need the plan before you stroll out with him," he hissed.

A prim-looking woman sniffed loudly. "Men. Always convinced they're the centre of the universe."

Another giggled. "Leave him alone. He's adorable."

Melicia rolled her eyes. "Focus, Keith. Sevins invited me to his place. I'll go with him. You and Ryan tail us—no matter what. Keep your distance, but don't lose sight."

Keith's jaw clenched. "I don't like it. Let's scrap this and lure him in here instead—get the truth out of him in the ladies' room."

"Really," Melicia said. "Do you expect him to carry a $20 million heirloom in his pocket?"

"Humph," Keith grumbled, pulling a face.

She softened her tone. "I know we have no choice. Just keep watch for me."

He exhaled sharply. "Okay. But if this goes south, I'm kicking his door down."

Melicia leaned in, cupping Keith's face with one hand before brushing her lips against his. "You're adorable. Has anyone ever told you that?" she teased, slipping her car keys into his palm as she pulled back.

The keys slid right through his fingers. Keith fumbled, bent to grab them, and managed to catch his shoe instead—sending him sprawling flat onto the tiles. The kiss had clearly rattled him.

Melicia stifled a laugh as she helped him back to his feet. "Smooth. Very smooth."

Keith kept his gaze fixed on the floor, his face burning crimson, while a few of the women in the washroom glanced his way—some blushing, others whispering behind their hands.

Melicia slid back to the table where Dr Sevins sat, and he looked up, smugness already in place. "All freshened up?" he asked, raising his glass.

She returned his smile like a knife disguised as silk. "Never better. Lead the way, Doctor."

He stood and guided her to the exit with a gentlemanly hand at the small of her back. Across the room, Keith and Ryan watched, two lumps of anxiety and poorly concealed bravery.

"I don't like the look of him," Ryan muttered, voice low. "Looks like the sort of chap who keeps a dungeon in the cellar."

Keith shoved the car keys into his pocket and shot Ryan a warning look. "Pipe down and keep your eyes on them. That's the job."

On the road, Sevins's sleek black motor purred ahead like a contented beast. Melicia sat beside him, playing the part with exquisite ease — a hand resting casually on his thigh, a laugh at the right moment, her attention feigned but perfectly timed as he rambled about exclusive clients and private appointments.

Behind them, Melicia's sports car snarled to life. Keith wrestled with the handling as he tried to stay on Sevins's tail. Ryan, cradling the dashboard like a talisman, squinted through the windscreen.

"Oi! Do you even know how to drive that thing properly?" Ryan hissed, white-knuckled.

Keith grinned despite the tremor in his hands. "Relax, Ryan. I've played enough racing games to get by."

Ryan gave a strangled groan. "This isn't some console, Keith. It's life — and I'm not keen on being a character in your terrible driving montage."

Keith pushed the accelerator a touch harder; the sports car leapt forward, Sevins's taillights a crimson dot ahead. "Then hold on. We're not letting her go in there alone."

Ryan sighed, a mix of panic and admiration. "You are insufferable."

Keith just kept his eyes on the road and the silhouette ahead. Tonight was too important to be taken lightly.

The city lights gave way to winding streets lined with iron gates and manicured hedges. Sevins's car glided into a secluded drive, the kind of place where secrets weren't just kept, but curated. The mansion loomed ahead, a sleek silhouette of glass and stone glowing faintly against the night. Too perfect. Too staged.

Inside the car, Melicia tilted her head, feigning admiration. "Quite the palace," she said lightly.

Sevins smirked as he eased to a stop. "A man needs his sanctuary. Privacy is priceless in my line of work."

Behind them, Keith cut the headlights and slowed to a crawl, pulling over just out of sight. Ryan's voice was taut. "That place looks like the set of a Bond villain's lair."

Keith's jaw tightened. "Which means we're right where we need to be." He reached for the door handle, but Ryan yanked at his sleeve.

"Wait. She said to follow, not crash the party."

Ahead, Melicia and Sevins stepped out. He placed a possessive hand at her waist, steering her toward the entrance. The mansion's sleek façade came alive — a discreet camera scanned Sevins's face and chimed a greeting. The heavy doors slid open with a smooth hiss.

Inside, the foyer came alive as heat sensors triggered soft pools of light. Sevins clapped once, and the brightness dimmed, replaced with a sultry wash of ambient glow. Music whispered through hidden speakers, a carefully curated soundtrack of sophistication and seduction.

Melicia let her lips part in a small, approving smile, masking her calculations.

Outside, Keith and Ryan crept closer, slipping behind a row of manicured shrubs. From there, they crouched low and peered through a panel of towering glass windows.

Keith's fists clenched against the grass. "I don't like this."

Ryan swallowed hard, eyes locked on the scene unfolding inside. "Yeah… me neither. But we're in it now."

Inside, the living room was a temple of wealth—featuring polished marble floors, walls lined with expensive antiques, and gilded frames that showcased oil paintings worthy of a museum. Sevins moved with casual arrogance, pouring two crystal glasses of brandy.

"Only the best for my guests," he said smoothly, handing one to Melicia.

She accepted, swirling the amber liquid but not drinking from it. Instead, she drifted to a wall of art, her heels clicking softly on the floor. Her eyes scanned the brushstrokes of a Renaissance piece, the gold leaf frame shimmering under the dimmed lights.

"These are remarkable," she said lightly, running her finger just shy of the canvas. "Auction houses, I'd guess?"

Sevins rose from the couch and strolled after her, his glass in hand. "You'd be correct. Sotheby's, Christie's… I don't buy to collect; I buy to own. There's a difference."

Melicia tilted her head, a slight grin tugging at her lips. "I suppose I just have a good eye for expensive things."

"You have good instincts, Melicia," Sevins said, his voice dropping lower as he stepped closer.

She glanced over her shoulder, her smile sharpening like a blade. "Instincts keep me alive in high society. I prefer the company of accomplished men." Her tone dripped with sarcasm, though she disguised it under a playful grin.

He chuckled, unfazed. "Then perhaps you've found the right company tonight."

She glided a few steps away, placing another antique vase between them like a shield. "Tell me about yourself, Doctor. What drives a man like you? Besides auctions and… flawless jawlines."

His eyes glittered, amused. "There's not much mystery. Privacy, power, the thrill of reinvention. That's what keeps me in demand."

Melicia let out a soft laugh, crossing to the opposite end of the room, ensuring the distance remained. "And how many women have you rehearsed that line for?"

"Not many," he said, following again, slower this time, as if stalking prey. "I don't usually bring women here. Especially not on a first date."

She turned, arching a brow. "So, I'm special, then?"

"You are," he admitted with a smile. "Though, truthfully… I broke that rule once before. And it didn't end well."

Her curiosity piqued. "What happened?"

The charm dropped from his face, replaced with a shadow. He set his glass down with a quiet clink. "She drugged me. Gagged me. Robbed me of something priceless. Vanished before dawn."

Melicia feigned sympathy, though her eyes flickered with calculation. "That's terrible. What was stolen?"

He waved a hand, dismissing. "Some things aren't meant to be shared over brandy. Let me show you what I have upstairs."

Meanwhile, outside, Keith and Ryan crouched beneath the living room's towering glass windows, watching like stranded spies. Ryan shifted nervously as the neighbour's dog started barking furiously, its paws scratching at the iron fence.

Ryan's eyes widened. "Oh no. Nope. That's my cue." He bolted back toward the car, muttering a string of curses.

Keith froze in place, caught in the glow of the house lights as the dog barked louder. He ducked lower, pressed to the wall, then made a desperate decision—grabbing the iron railing of the side window and hauling himself upward. His shoes scraped against the glass as he scrambled for footing.

Inside, Sevins's head snapped toward the sound. "What was that?" He strode toward the window, suspicion flaring.

Melicia's pulse spiked. Without missing a beat, she slid into his path, her hand brushing his arm. "Tell me, Doctor," she purred, forcing his gaze back to her, "do you really use all these rehearsed stories to impress women? Or just the ones you want to keep around?"

His expression softened again, diverted by her teasing grin. He smiled, almost flattered. "Only for the ones worth breaking my rules."

Her laughter rang out like music, though her mind was already racing. Upstairs. Secrets. Keith is in trouble. She just had to keep Sevins close—and distracted—long enough for Keith to find what they came for.

Dr Sevins stood at the bottom of the staircase, one hand resting on the polished bannister. "Come," he said, voice low, almost coaxing. "Upstairs, I'll show you my real treasures. What I keep here in the living room is just for guests."

Melicia tilted her head, her lips curling in a playful grin. "Real treasures? My, you make it sound like a dragon's lair." She didn't move. Instead, she stepped toward another framed painting on the wall, tracing the edge of the gilded frame with her finger. "Or is it another auction piece you 'rescued' from an unsuspecting bidder?"

Sevins chuckled, though his eyes stayed sharp on her. "You have a sharp tongue, Melicia. Dangerous in the wrong company." He came closer, the faint smell of brandy lingering on him.

"Dangerous?" she repeated, turning to face him with mock innocence. "Or intoxicating?"

Just then, outside, Keith's foot slipped on the window railing. He gasped, clawing at the sill, his shoe scraping noisily against the wall. A loose flowerpot tipped and crashed down below.

Sevins froze. His head snapped toward the window. Melicia's heart lurched, but she forced herself to stay calm. She stepped into his line of sight, blocking his view. "Paranoid, Doctor?" she teased, her hand brushing against his sleeve. "You hear ghosts, too?"

Sevins narrowed his eyes, studying her, but her mischievous grin disarmed him. Slowly, he turned back. "You distract too easily," he said, amused.

"Only when I'm bored," she shot back. "Tell me—how many women have you lured here with promises of rare collections and priceless art?"

His smile tightened. "You're only the second."

"Oh?" She raised a brow, leaning closer, though keeping her body angled away. "And what happened to the first?"

For the first time, his face darkened. "She made a mistake. Tried to rob me." His jaw clenched. "I don't take betrayal lightly."

From the window, Keith's head appeared, red-faced, straining as he finally hauled himself halfway inside. He dared not breathe.

Melicia's eyes flicked toward Sevins, masking her panic with another sly grin. "You must frighten women off with that charming tone. Or… maybe you frighten yourself?"

Sevins studied her, then smirked. "You have courage, Melicia. I like that." He extended his hand toward her. "Upstairs. I insist."

She glanced at his hand but didn't take it. Instead, she pivoted toward another painting, her voice light but her steps keeping distance.

Sevins' patience wavered, but before he could press further, the faint creak of a floorboard upstairs broke the silence. Both froze.

Melicia's pulse spiked. Keith, you idiot.

Sevins' gaze shot upward. "What was that?"

Melicia quickly slid closer, placing a hand on his chest, forcing his attention back to her. "Maybe your ghost again, Doctor," she whispered, eyes locking on his. "Or maybe… It's just me."

Dr Sevins' hand tightened on Melicia's wrist as he guided her upstairs. "Come," he said silkily, "you'll see what separates me from every other man you've ever met."

Melicia rolled her eyes just enough for him not to see. God, these men are all the same. Still, she let him lead her, her heels clicking against the polished wood.

At the end of the corridor, Sevins pressed his thumb against a biometric scanner and keyed in a code. The door hissed open. Inside was a gallery—walls covered with glossy photographs, some framed, some pinned like trophies. Politicians, film stars, CEOs, models—all of them with perfect jawlines, flawless noses, sculpted cheekbones.

"Voilà." Sevins spread his arms proudly. "Every masterpiece here has felt my touch."

Melicia arched a brow. "Your touch? Interesting way to describe carving people's faces with a scalpel."

Sevins laughed, unfazed. "It's art, my dear. And you—" he stepped closer, lowering his voice—"you could be perfection itself, if you'd let me. A stronger chin, higher cheekbones. Imagine what doors would open for you…"

Melicia smirked, sidestepping him. "I'm flattered. But trust me, Doctor, the doors I want are already open."

Meanwhile, in the lavish bedroom, Keith tiptoed inside, rifling through drawers and cabinets. His heart hammered. Where is it? Where is it? He pulled open a jewellery box—pearls, emeralds, rubies—nothing that looked like an heirloom. Then he heard voices approaching.

"Crap." He dove under the bed just as Sevins pushed the door open with a flourish.

"Here," Sevins said, sweeping a hand across his vast bedroom. "The true heart of my sanctuary. Only very special women make it this far."

Melicia chuckled dryly. "Lucky me."

Keith, under the bed, held his breath as Melicia's heels clicked dangerously close. Dust tickled his nose. Don't sneeze. Don't sneeze. Don't— "Achoo!"

Sevins froze. “What was that?” Melicia laughed quickly, waving it off. “My perfume. Makes me sneeze sometimes. Don’t tell me your genius hasn’t cured allergies yet.”

Sevins smirked, relaxing again. “Not yet. But perhaps… a drink will help?”

Meanwhile, downstairs…

Ryan crept in through a side window, landing with a soft thud. He looked around nervously. “Keith? Keith, where are you?” he whispered, crawling along the floor like a burglar who’d lost his nerve.

Then his eyes caught the glittering bar counter. Bottles of every brand imaginable, glowing like treasure under LED lights. His jaw dropped. “Holy… this guy has Glenfiddich 50. And—wait—is that Louis XIII cognac?”

He forgot entirely about stealth. “Well, it’d be rude not to taste-test…” One sip became two. Two became five. Soon, Ryan was slouched against the counter, happily mixing cocktails like a bartender at his own wedding.

Back upstairs…

Sevins leaned in too close, brushing Melicia’s arm. “Stay tonight. I’ll make it worth your while.”

Melicia’s smile sharpened. “Doctor, I said I like men of accomplishment. Not men who mistake themselves for peacocks.”

When he reached for her waist, she moved lightning-fast—grabbing his wrist, spinning, and slamming him flat on the floor with a judo throw. The thud echoed through the room.

“Argh! My back!” Sevins yelped, writhing.

Melicia pinned his arm, her voice low and sharp. “Enough games. Where’s the heirloom you bought from Diggers?”

His eyes widened in panic. “Who…what?”

At that moment, Keith shuffled out from under the bed, dust clinging to his hair, his expression caught somewhere between guilty and sheepish.

Sevins gaped. “And you—what the hell? Who are you people?”

Keith froze, hands half-raised. “Uh… plumber. Bed plumber. Just… checking the springs.”

Melicia’s glare could have cut steel. “Did you find the safe?”

Keith blinked. “What safe?”

Melicia closed her eyes, pinched the bridge of her nose, and exhaled slowly. When she looked back at him, her expression was pure fury wrapped in disbelief. “Seriously.”

Of course, she knew Keith could be naïve, but she hadn’t expected this level of it. Where did he think priceless possessions went—on a nightstand with the car keys? She bit back the urge to scream, forcing herself to keep her composure.

Instead, she shifted her focus back to Sevins, her hand tightening on his arm, twisting it just enough to make him hiss in pain. Her voice was calm, deliberate.

“The heirloom. From Star Pawn. Where is it?”

“I-I don’t know what you’re talking about!” Sevins gasped, panic rising in his chest. “If this is a robbery, fine—take whatever you want! … leave the nose intact!”

Melicia's hand snapped across his cheek, a sharp sting rather than real harm. "Focus, Doctor. We're not here for your rhinoplasty portfolio. We want the heirloom."

His breathing grew ragged; his shoulders sagging, he finally relented. "Alright… fine. I bought it. Ten million, off a black-market bid. But it's gone."

Keith's brows knitted. "Gone? What the hell do you mean, gone?"

Sevins groaned, sitting on the edge of the bed, rubbing his arm. "I gave it to a woman. My girlfriend at the time. She… well, she ran off with it."

Melicia crossed her arms. "Let me guess. Another special woman who got this far upstairs?"

Sevins winced. "Touché."

Keith leaned in. "Name. We need a name."

Sevins hesitated, then sighed. "Diana. Diana Rods."

At that exact moment, Ryan stumbled in from the stairs, glass in hand, grinning like an idiot. "Guys, you have to try the Scotch downstairs—oh, hey, is this the bedroom?"

Melicia facepalmed. Keith groaned. Sevins blinked. "…Are you all insane?"

Melicia stood tall, ignoring the chaos around her. "Doctor. Talk when you are asked to."

Sevins managed a shaky grin despite everything. "For a woman who just threw me across my own floor… I think I might be in love."

Melicia rolled her eyes. "Of course you are."

"Tell us about Diana Rods," Keith said. His voice had gone flat—no warmth, no patience, just business.

Sevins swallowed hard and fumbled for his phone. His knees still wobbled from the earlier fall, and he steadied himself on the edge of the bed. After a few frantic swipes, he found the photo and held the screen out with a shaky hand.

"Here… that's her."

The woman in the picture was striking—high cheekbones, glossy hair, the kind of beauty that made people pause mid-sentence in casinos or galleries. Ryan let out a low whistle before his brain caught up.

"She's hot," he blurted, far too loudly.

Keith smacked his arm. "Ryan. Shut it."

Melicia leaned in, her gaze cutting straight through Sevins. "Where do we find her?"

He dragged a hand down his face, sweat beading along his hairline. "I don't know. I tried. She changed her number, moved out, disappeared completely." His voice warbled between apology and annoyance. "One woman robs me, another slaps me—hell of an evening."

Melicia's smile was thin and lethal. "Listen carefully," she said, her voice soft in the way knives are soft. "You breathe a word of tonight to anyone—anyone—and we'll make sure your 'discreet clients' become very public knowledge. Some of them won't appreciate the exposure."

Whatever colour Sevins had left drained out of him. "You wouldn't—"

Her look finished the sentence for him.

Ryan, still unsteady, tugged at his jacket like he was attempting dignity. "Right, brilliant. Lovely evening, Doctor. Try not to die of shame."

The three of them edged toward the door. Before stepping out, Melicia cast Sevins one last cool, warning glance. "We'll be in touch."

The door thudded shut behind them, leaving Sevins alone in the humming stillness of his own mansion. He sagged back onto the bed, staring blankly at the wood panels.

A second later, his phone clattered against the covers—small, embarrassed, and much too loud in the empty room. He had arrived expecting flirtation and an easy night; instead, he'd been interrogated, threatened, and left with a sour knot of regret twisting in his gut.

Out on the driveway, the three descended the broad steps. Keith jingled the car keys in his hand, Ryan mumbled under his breath, and Melicia stared straight ahead.

They slipped into their cars and pulled away into the night, each carrying a different weight: Melicia's urgency sharpened into resolve, Keith's throat tightened with unease, and Ryan—well, he clung to the thought that if this somehow succeeded, he might finally have something worth adding to his otherwise pitiful CV.

The ride back was quiet at first, the city's late-night streets passing in a blur of sodium lights. Ryan finally broke the silence, slumping against the window with a sigh.

"Can't believe it," he muttered. "For a second, I thought tonight was it. We were right there—thought we had the heirloom in our hands."

Melicia rubbed her temple; frustration etched into her face. "Instead, we wasted hours chasing a dead end. And Sevins? He's nothing but a rich collector who's already lost track of what he bought."

Keith tightened his grip on the wheel. "We don't have hours to waste. Van gave us forty-eight. After tonight, we're down to thirty-six."

That hung in the air, heavy.

Ryan shook his head. "So now what? Who the hell is Diana Rod anyway? Never even heard the name."

Melicia's eyes narrowed, staring out the window as if the night itself might give her answers. "Whoever she is, she's got it. And if Sevins lost it to her, then she's either dangerous or stupidly lucky. Either way—we find her, we find the heirloom."

Keith exhaled slowly, a hard edge in his voice. "Here we go again."

A hush settled over them, thick with unspoken thoughts, broken only by the low drone of the car engine as it wound through the city toward home.

When they arrived at the apartment, the streets outside had fallen silent, and the city lulled into a late-night calm. Melicia slipped into her bedroom, the door clicking shut behind her. Guilt gnawed at her—she knew the stakes. If they failed to secure the heirloom, Keith and Ryan would pay the price for her mistake. Van, the ruthless billionaire, would see to that, his tyranny sparing no one.

Ryan, his stomach rumbling and mind hazy from too many glasses of Sevin's champagne, raided the kitchen for a late-night snack. With a satisfied grunt, he sprawled across the couch, still in his shoes, and succumbed to a restless sleep.

Keith lingered outside Melicia's door, his hand hovering as if to knock, words he couldn't quite form weighing on him. Instead, he retreated, stepping into the spare bedroom next to hers. He closed the door softly, and soon, the night's burdens pulled him into a heavy, dreamless sleep.

Hours later, soft as breath, Melicia's door creaked open. Barefoot, she crossed the short hall and eased into Keith's room. He didn't stir when she slid beneath the blanket, curling into the warmth of his side. By the time dawn thinned the dark, Keith shifted, half-dreaming, and realised she was there. Without thinking, he pulled her close. She responded in kind, nestling into his chest as both drifted back into a deeper sleep.

The sun broke through the blinds, warming the room. Keith woke first. Careful not to disturb her, he slipped away, finding Ryan sprawled across the living room couch. Shaking his head with a faint smile, Keith turned to the kitchen.

A while later, he returned with a tray—coffee, toast, eggs still steaming. Setting it on the nightstand, he leaned down and brushed a kiss against Melicia's cheek. Her eyes fluttered open, confusion melting into a smile when she saw the breakfast waiting for her.

"You made this?" she murmured, voice rough with sleep.

Keith nodded, a quiet grin tugging at his lips. "Couldn't let you start the day hungry."

She sat up slowly, hair tangled, but her smile lingered—softer, warmer than Keith had ever seen.

Chapter 11

Rusty Halo

The room was still warm from the morning sun. Keith had cleared away the breakfast tray, but the faint smell of toast and coffee lingered in the air. Melicia sat at the edge of the bed, her back straight, but her hands restless, twisting the sheets into tiny knots.

Keith noticed. He leaned against the doorframe, arms folded, his voice calm. "You want to tell me what's on your mind?"

Her lips pressed into a line before she gave a small, humourless laugh. "Careful, Keith. When I open up, people usually run the other way."

"Try me," he said.

That disarmed her more than she expected. She sighed, tugged at a loose thread on the blanket, and began.

"You know, I wasn't born into this life. The schemes, the lies, the games—I learned them. But before all that… I had what most people call a perfect life."

Keith tilted his head. “Perfect?”

She nodded slowly. “Wealthy father. He was respected —a man who dined with politicians and business giants. My mother? She looked like she stepped out of a magazine—flawless, admired, adored by everyone who didn’t live under the same roof.” Her smile turned bitter. “To the world, she was a role model. To us kids, she was a ghost. Too busy being perfect to notice her family rotting inside.”

Keith said nothing, just letting her words spill.

“My brother… he was the storm in that perfect house. Drugs, alcohol, fights in back alleys—he treated life like a dare. The law caught him more times than I can count. And every time, he promised he’d change.” She shook her head slowly. “But promises don’t mean much when you’re drowning yourself.”

Her voice dropped lower. “The night it happened… I was sixteen. He climbed through my bedroom window. His face was pale, his hands shaking. He’d robbed a man—stupid, reckless. He swore if they caught him again, he’d go straight to prison. He begged me, Keith. Begged like his life depended on it.”

Keith leaned forward, resting his elbows on his knees. “And you believed him.”

“I wanted to.” Her laugh cracked. “I loved him. He was my brother. So, I said it was me. I told the police I did it. They arrested me. Prison—thirty days that felt like thirty years. A year of community service. Do you know what the worst part was?”

Keith shook his head.

“My parents believed it. They thought I was the bad one all along. The black sheep, the stain on their reputation. After everything… I thought maybe my brother would straighten out. That my sacrifice would mean something."

Her voice faltered, but she didn't stop. "But he didn't. He got into a bar fight months later. Landed in prison anyway. All I did was destroy myself for nothing. My parents never forgave me. They washed their hands of me. I walked out of that house and never looked back."

Keith's jaw tightened. "You were sixteen. You carried someone else's sins on your shoulders. That doesn't make you the stain—it makes you stronger than all of them combined."

She gave him a sharp look, eyes glassy. "Stronger? Keith, I wasn't strong—I was lost. After I finished community service, I had nowhere to go. No home. No family. I thought… maybe I could cheat the world before it cheated me. I tried a con—my first real one. And guess what? I got caught."

Keith frowned, leaning in.

"They sent me back. Three months this time. And that's when I met her." Melicia's tone shifted—softer, almost reverent. "She called herself Florist. No one knew her real name. She had been inside for years, but she managed to make the prison garden bloom like a paradise. Roses, lilies, things I'd never seen before. She said Flowers don't lie, only people do."

Her lips curved faintly. "She took me under her wing. Taught me the first rule: don't get caught. She showed me how to watch, how to listen, how to slip through cracks. She said survival wasn't about strength—it was about strategy. About knowing when to play the fool and when to play the wolf."

Keith's eyes softened. "And you listened."

"I listened. I learned. And when I walked out the second time, I never looked back." Her gaze dropped, voice quieter now. "The last time I saw her… I brought her flowers. She wouldn't even take them. She told me never to visit again. Said emotions were chains, and chains get you caught. She didn't want me tied to her, or anyone. 'Cut your heart out, Melicia, if you want to survive.' Those were her words."

The silence stretched. Keith exhaled slowly. "And you've been surviving ever since."

She looked at him then, really looked him in the eye. "Surviving, yes. Living? I don't know. Sometimes I wonder if Florist was right. Emotions… they do get you hurt."

Keith didn't look away. "Or maybe they make the fight worth it."

Something flickered across her face—doubt, fear, maybe even longing. She turned her gaze aside, afraid of what she might let slip if she held his eyes too long.

In that moment, Keith understood exactly what she'd handed him — not a story to tuck away, but her trust. That was worth more than any heirloom. He eased out of the bedroom, leaving Melicia curled inwards, a slight, private silhouette of thought.

For the first time since he'd known her, she looked vulnerable: hair loose at the temple, shoulders slightly hunched as if the walls she'd spent years building had finally cracked. He closed the door on soft hinges and leaned his back against it, chest tight with everything unsaid.

His phone felt heavier than it ought to. He stared at the screen, his thumb hovering over a number he did not want to dial. One breath. Two. He pressed call.

Three rings, then a crisp, slightly groggy voice: "Officer Leann."

"This is Keith," he said, keeping his tone low.

A pause, then recognition. “Keith. You pick strange hours to call — I was about to head back home.”

Keith let out a dry chuckle. “I need help. I didn’t know who to turn to.”

Leann’s suspicion woke instantly. “I can hear the desperation. What’s going on?”

“I need information. Fast. About a woman named Diana Rod.”

Silence stretched — sharp, probing. “Why do I have the feeling this involves her?”

“Because it does. Melicia’s with me.”

Leann’s breath snagged; her voice tightened. “I knew it. I knew she wasn’t dead. Couldn’t prove it — but damn it, Keith, I knew.”

“Leann, listen.” Keith’s tone snapped with urgency. “I’ll explain later. For now — Diana Rod. Everything you’ve got.”

Officer Leann gets back to her seat, opens her machine.

There was the faint clatter of keys. “Diana Rod… petty theft, cons, laundering — small-time trouble on paper. Off the record? She’s been Van’s errand girl for years. His shadow. She moves for him when he doesn’t want his fingerprints on a job.”

Keith felt the phone bite into his palm. “So, she works for him.”

“You know Van?” Leann’s voice sharpened.

“Sort of,” Keith said. “We had an unpleasant encounter earlier.”

“Goodness. What have you dragged yourself into? Van is not someone to mess with.”

Keith swallowed. "Long story. Melicia stole a family heirloom from Van. He found out. She faked her death to get away. Now I'm helping her return it before he decides neither of us is worth keeping."

Leann was quiet for a beat, then her verdict landed. "Van's playing you. If Diana has it, it's either because he told her to hold it — or she's trying to cut herself a bigger slice. Either way, nothing she does stays off his radar for long."

Melicia appeared in the hallway like she'd materialised from the shadows — arms crossed, eyes razor-sharp. She looked at Keith with that same expression she reserved for betrayals.

Keith didn't hang up. He lowered the phone but left it to his ear.

"What is it?" she asked, voice low, steel under the surface.

He hit the speaker. Leann's voice filled the quiet room. "Your Diana isn't just a petty thief. She's Van's shadow. If Van told you to fetch the heirloom, think: why send Melicia after something he already knows where to find? Either he's testing you — or he's setting a trap."

Melicia's colour drained. Her jaw tightened. "So, it's a trap. All of it."

At that moment, Ryan stumbled out of the bathroom — hair a mess, eyes rimmed red, rubbing his head. He squinted at the tableau like someone who'd wandered into a wake.

"Why does everyone look like they've seen a ghost?" he muttered.

No one answered. The room felt smaller, as if Van's presence pressed in from outside, making every movement riskier.

"You're a lifesaver, Officer Leann," Keith said, relief finally cutting through.

"Stay out of trouble, Keith," Leann replied, softer now. "You're not as expendable as you think. Call me if anything changes."

The line went dead. Keith slid the phone into his pocket and let out a breath, as if exhaling could lighten the load.

"We need a plan," he said, turning to Melicia and Ryan.

Ryan, still half-limping on the sofa like a man recovering from a beating, perked up at the word plan. He sniffed the air theatrically. "So — what's the plan? Do I seduce Diana and save the day? Always happy to sacrifice myself for the cause."

Melicia's glare could have stripped the wallpaper. "Shut it, Ryan. Seriously — or I'll feed you to the lions."

Ryan grinned, unbothered. "They won't eat me. Too stringy. And besides, I've got a face for radio — they'd die laughing first."

Keith pinched the bridge of his nose; patience was thinning. "No jokes. We have less than twenty-four hours. We track Diana, find the heirloom, and figure out where her loyalties lie. If she's still running for Van, confronting her directly is suicide."

Melicia leaned forward, voice low and razor-sharp. "We're looking at three scenarios. One: Diana's gone rogue and kept the heirloom. Two: she's still Van's courier, meaning he already knows where it is and is manipulating us. Three: Van's staging a test — or a trap — to see who blinks."

Ryan dropped his face into his hands and groaned. "Brilliant. All of them sound like different flavours of execution."

Melicia rose smoothly and walked to the bedroom. At the doorway, she paused and glanced back with a cold, small smile. "Go clean up. We move in an hour. We'll need sharp minds and cleaner faces." The door clicked shut, leaving Keith and Ryan staring at each other in the hush.

"For the record," Ryan muttered, "I still vote seduction."

Keith's glare did the rest of the talking.

Chapter 12

Heels, Trouble, and Two Idiots

Keith and Ryan emerged from the bedroom like two battle-worn soldiers preparing for one last mission. Ryan had somehow managed to make his shirt three shades louder than before and looked as if he'd accidentally bathed in aftershave. Keith, on the other hand, was the complete opposite—sharp suit, polished shoes, every detail in place. He knew Melicia would expect nothing less. They couldn't afford to mess this up.

Settling onto the sofa, they waited—silent, focused, and pretending not to smell the cloud of Ryan's cologne hanging in the air.

"What's keeping her?" Ryan whined after two interminable minutes. He jiggled his knee, tapping a nervous rhythm. "She's been in there ages. Has she turned into Cinderella or what?"

Keith didn't answer. He was watching the bedroom door as if it might open and present the answer with a bow. The silence stretched until he couldn't stand it. He swung himself up and padded across to the door, hand raised to knock — and it opened before he could.

Melicia stood framed in the doorway like something out of an advert: hair loose, dress neat and striking, yet somehow effortless. She had the sort of look that stopped conversation mid-word. Keith's mouth went dry.

"Well, my husband, shall we?" she said, with a teasing lift to her eyebrow that made Keith feel simultaneously proud and ridiculous.

"Right," Ryan said, recovering the only wit he had left. "Big day for the married couple. When did this happen? I must have missed the invite."

Melicia gave him an incredible smile, then turned and drifted past. Keith followed as if in a trance. They spilt out to the drive and slid into her car—Keith in the passenger seat, Ryan sulking into the back like a displaced monarch.

Melicia started the engine, and the car came to life. She didn't potter. The car accelerated with the confident impatience of someone who knew every turn. Streetlights smeared into streaks. The city thinned, houses dissolved into hedges, and the motorway opened like a ribbon to the outskirts.

Keith clutched the grab handle above the door so hard his knuckles blanched. "So… er, what's the plan?" he asked, voice a notch higher than usual. The speed made him sound like a man trying to remain calm on a roller coaster.

"We're going to the old people's home," Melicia said without looking at him, one hand on the wheel, the other tapping the steering column in time to the radio.

Ryan sat up, all alarm. "The what now? Older adults' home? Is this—are we visiting your nan in disguise?"

"No," Melicia replied, glassy-eyed with amusement. "Diana Rods visits her mother there every Thursday. I've been told she'll be there today."

Keith blinked. "Diana Rods — the one with the heirloom? How do you know she goes to a care home?"

Melicia allowed a tiny, secretive grin. "Let's say I have a source. People with jobs, eyes, and occasionally morals." She flicked an annoyed look at Ryan.

Ryan made a sound somewhere between a growl and a sob. "Kidnap her mother? No. I did not sign up for a retirement-home abduction scheme. I like my freedom, thank you very much. I have a following on social media to maintain."

Melicia's expression softened only a fraction. "We are not kidnapping anyone, Ryan. Calm down. This is straightforward: we mingle. Blend in. I walk up to Diana as an acquaintance; Keith plays the concerned neighbour or an overly affectionate nephew — whatever makes the staff relax. You keep watch, help with small talk, and for heaven's sake, don't flirt with the receptionist."

Ryan sat bolt upright, affronted. "Flirt? Who, me? I was never going to—okay, maybe a little. But only to distract, tactical flirting. For the mission."

Keith let out a short, incredulous laugh. "Tactical flirting. Right. Because that always ends well."

Melicia shot him a look. "Listen — we don't confront Diana. We find out where she goes after visiting time. We watch who meets her. We listen to names, watch hands, count cars. No drama, no force. If Diana's got the heirloom, she'll slip up. People who steal for a living aren't as careful with people they think are harmless."

Ryan chewed the inside of his cheek. "And if she's playing us? If she's working for Van and this whole thing is—" he made a vague, cinematic gesture, "—a distraction while Van sneaks up behind us with a chainsaw or whatever it is he does?"

"Then we have a contingency," Melicia said, voice steady. "But first, we go in like normal folk. I'll be the pretty face. Keith, you're the puzzled neighbour who can't find his bus pass. Ryan, you be… well, you be mildly annoying in a charming way. And keep your phone on silent."

Keith felt his stomach do a small somersault. "You're seriously asking me to play a relative?" he said, half-pleading, half-amused.

"You're better at being earnest," Melicia replied. "Trust me."

The car slowed as they turned into the lane that led to the care home. The building looked gentler than the word suggested: low brick, tidy flowerbeds, a line of wheelchairs parked like gossiping aunts beneath the windows. A couple of residents sat in the courtyard under blankets as a nurse pushed a tea trolley. The smell of cut grass and lemon disinfectant mingled oddly in the air.

"And remember," Melicia added as they pulled up, engine ticking as it cooled, "if anyone asks, we're mundane. No interesting histories, no dramatic pasts. We're two thoughtful visitors who've popped in by chance."

Ryan hopped out first, doing a slight, exaggerated stretch. "Right. Mundane. Got it. I can do mundane. Mostly."

The three of them stepped out together, Melicia's presence somehow both incongruous and natural among the tidy rows of geraniums. Keith couldn't help glancing at her — at the way she adjusted her jacket, the steadiness of her breath. He'd followed her into this because he believed in her, even when the path looked utterly absurd.

"Stay close," Melicia whispered as the sun dipped a little lower and the front door of the home opened like a promise. "Eyes open. Play the part. And for goodness' sake, Ryan — no spontaneous serenading."

Ryan mouthed, "No promises," but his grin was sheepish rather than serious. They stepped inside, the automatic doors whispering shut behind them, and the afternoon reshaped itself around their little, risky choreography.

The glass doors whispered open as they stepped inside.

Whatever Keith had expected from a "care home," it wasn't this.

Soft classical music drifted through the air. The floor gleamed like marble, reflecting golden light from an ornate chandelier overhead. A faint scent of lilies and disinfectant mingled in a strange harmony. The reception counter stood ahead—polished wood, manned by a woman in a cream blazer who smiled with professional warmth.

But what caught Keith's eye wasn't the decor. It was the sheer security.

Two guards in navy suits lingered discreetly near the elevators, earpieces coiled tight against their necks, walkie-talkies clipped to their belts. Their sidearms—bayonets, of all things—gleamed faintly under the lights. Nurses moved with crisp precision down the hallway, carrying tablets instead of clipboards.

Ryan let out a low whistle. "I've seen hotels with less sparkle. What's this place, the Ritz for retirees?"

Keith murmured under his breath, "How on earth can Diana afford this? Her mother's care alone must cost a fortune."

Melicia's eyes darted across the lobby, quick and assessing. "Let's not lose focus," she said. Her tone was calm, but Keith caught the edge of curiosity beneath it.

They moved toward the front desk, trying to blend in. Melicia straightened her jacket, her heels tapping softly against the floor.

"I'll do the talking," she whispered.

Keith nodded. "You always do."

Melicia approached the receptionist with the kind of poise that could charm a border guard. "Good afternoon," she began smoothly, flashing a practised smile. "I'm here to visit a resident—Mrs. Rods. I believe she's in the west wing?"

The receptionist glanced at her tablet, scrolling through it. "Are you family?"

Before Melicia could answer the receptionist, Keith's gaze snagged on a blur of motion by the far glass doors. He went still.

There—pushing a wheelchair toward the exit—was Diana.

She was disarmingly composed in a bottle-green coat, hair tied back, sunglasses perched on her head like a small crown. A calm, practised smile framed her face as she guided the frail woman in the chair. It wasn't serenity Keith saw in that smile; it was control. Control was Diana's trade.

"Keith?" Melicia asked, her voice cutting across the lobby's murmur. "What is it?"

He didn't answer. His pulse had switched from steady to sprint.

Diana reached the main door; sunlight spilt over her shoulder. Keith moved before he'd decided to—slipping past two bemused visitors and a nurse pushing a medicine trolley, not noticing the startled looks as he fell through the automatic doors.

Back inside, Ryan lounged by the coffee machine, watching a passing nurse like a man appreciating fine art. "This place could use more young male patients," he observed, smirking.

Melicia watched Keith disappear through the glass. "Oh, brilliant," she muttered.

Ryan blinked. "Where's lover-boy off to now?"

"Following trouble," Melicia said, rubbing her temples. "He's spotted Diana."

Ryan's smirk dropped. "You've got to be joking. That's her?"

"The one and only," Melicia said.

Ryan's grin faded into something less confident. "Oh. We're so dead."

Outside, the air was cleaner—sharper. Diana was helping her mother out of the wheelchair, letting her stretch her legs among the neatly trimmed rose bushes. The older woman smiled faintly, leaning on her daughter's arm. But she couldn't stand for long, and soon Diana was struggling to guide her gently back into the chair.

Keith paused nearby, pretending to admire the garden. He took a slow breath, trying to look casual—a man enjoying the afternoon breeze, not a man stalking a ghost from his past.

Then, with the confidence of someone who had absolutely no plan, he straightened his collar and walked over. "Need a hand?" he asked lightly. Without waiting for an answer, he stepped in to help Diana ease her mother back into the wheelchair.

Diana turned, her gaze cool and assessing. No recognition flickered in her eyes—just polite curiosity. "I'm sorry," she said smoothly. "Do I know you?"

Keith chuckled, stepping closer. "Not yet. But fate seems to enjoy these kinds of coincidences."

She tilted her head, a faint smirk tugging at her lips. "Smooth talker. Do you always wait by hospital exits for fate to show up in heels?"

"Only when fate looks like you," Keith shot back with a grin.

Diana laughed—a soft, melodic sound that made Keith's chest tighten despite himself. There was warmth in it, but something else too. Something deliberate.

"Fine, Romeo," she said, handing him the wheelchair handles. "You can push her then. But keep up—I don't like slow men."

Keith took the handles, steadying himself. "I'll take that as a challenge."

As they strolled down the path, Diana glanced sideways. "So, tell me, why exactly are you helping me?"

"Well," Keith said, improvising, "I saw you struggling. Thought I'd be a gentleman."

"Ah. A gentleman and a flirt," she teased. "That's a dangerous mix."

Keith smiled. "Depends who's on the receiving end."

Her mother smiled vaguely, unaware of the tension humming between them. Diana kept her gaze forward. "So, what brings you here? Have we met before?"

"I'm visiting my aunt," Keith replied smoothly. "First time, actually. I wasn't too keen on coming—but you know how women can be. They insist, and we follow."

"Are we referring to your wife?" she asked, one brow lifting.

Keith smirked. "My wife passed away in a road accident. These days, I seem to be haunted by another woman from the afterlife."

That earned a small laugh from Diana—light, amused, curious. "You're an interesting man, Mr…?"

"Keith," he said quickly.

"I'm sure I've seen you somewhere before," she murmured, squinting slightly. "I never forget a face."

Keith grinned. "That's because I tend to leave an impression."

"Ah," she said. "Confident too. Dangerous combination."

Across the courtyard, Melicia and Ryan lurked near the vending machine, trying (and failing) to look inconspicuous.

Ryan popped a chip into his mouth. "Is he… flirting?"

Melicia's jaw tightened. "He thinks he's gathering intel. I think he's auditioning for a bad romance film."

Ryan snorted mid-chew, nearly choking. "He's actually not bad. Look—she's laughing!"

Melicia rolled her eyes. "Laughing before poisoning him, maybe."

Ryan leaned in. "Want me to wingman?"

Melicia's glare could've frozen lava. "You so much as breathe in their direction, and I'll feed you to Van myself."

Ryan raised both hands. "Copy that, boss lady."

They watched as Keith and Diana continued walking toward the parking lot, chatting like old flames who hadn't met yet. Melicia's instincts screamed—Diana wasn't flirting, she was playing. And Melicia had seen enough cons to know that Keith was about to walk straight into one.

Diana handed her mother over to the nurse, her movements smooth and composed. When she turned back, Keith was standing awkwardly by the corridor railing, silently rehearsing his following line like a student before an oral exam.

"You've been very helpful," she said sweetly, her tone laced with something playful. "Let me thank you properly. Dinner, maybe?"

Keith blinked. "Dinner?"

She leaned in slightly, her perfume brushing against his neck like a whisper. "You don't say no to a lady, do you?"

He smirked. "Depends on the lady."

"Good. Then it's a yes."

Without waiting for a reply, Diana walked away, her heels clicking softly against the pavement. Keith watched her glide toward a sleek silver sedan parked nearby. She got in, gave him one last glance through the window, and drove off.

A moment later, Melicia and Ryan appeared from behind a parked car, grinning like proud parents watching their kid pull off a miracle.

"So, Romeo," Melicia teased, folding her arms. "Didn't know you had that in you."

Ryan clapped Keith on the shoulder. "Man, you were smooth! What did you even say? She looked like she'd known you for years."

Melicia narrowed her eyes. "Don't get too comfortable. She's onto us, I can feel it."

Keith ran a hand through his hair, still half dazed. "Well… she invited me to dinner."

Ryan burst out laughing. "Now that's what I call killer instinct. Keith, you've got it!"

"Don't hold your horses just yet," Melicia cut in, her tone cooling the air. "Something about this doesn't sit right."

Ryan shrugged. "Fine, detective. What's our next move?"

Melicia smirked faintly. "We head home. Get lover boy ready for his date."

Keith exhaled, half a laugh, half a sigh. "Yeah. Let's hope I don't end up being the one who gets played."

Chapter 13

Flirt First, Panic Later

Keith stands before the tall mirror near the window, adjusting his tie for the fourth time. The new tailored suit fits too well — clean lines, crisp shoulders — making him look like a man with more confidence than he feels.

Ryan lounges on the couch, one sock off, munching on chips he found somewhere in the kitchen. He watches Keith like a proud parent watching a kid go to prom.

"Man, if she doesn't fall for you, she's legally blind," Ryan grins, crumbs flying.

"Let's just hope she talks more than she flirts," Keith answers without looking up, still fixing his cufflinks.

"Why? You can't handle competition?" Ryan teases, kicking his feet up on the coffee table.

"No," Keith smirks faintly. "I just don't like being played."

Before Ryan can respond, Melicia emerges from the bedroom — calm, composed, dressed in casual black with her hair pulled back. In her hand, a tiny earpiece glints under the light.

"Wear this," she holds it out to Keith. "I'll be listening. If she mentions Van, the heirloom, anything, I want to know right away."

Keith hesitates, meeting her gaze. "You don't trust me?"

"I don't trust her. There's a difference."

Their eyes hold for a beat too long — a silence thick enough to be heard. Keith finally takes the earpiece and slips it on.

"Alright, lovebirds, let's not make this weird. Some of us are single and sensitive." Ryan mutters, raising his chip bag like a toast.

Melicia shoots him a death glare. "Ryan, you're coming with me. We'll follow them."

"Ah, great. My dream date — a stakeout with you." Ryan groans, grabbing his jacket.

"You talk too much," she replies dryly, heading for the door.

Ryan closes the door behind them.

They pile into the car, and Melicia takes off like she's chasing the apocalypse. Ryan and Keith clutch the seats, half-praying, half-regretting every life choice that led them here. Only when she eases off the gas do they remember to breathe.

The black car glides to a stop at the curb. Ahead, the restaurant gleams — all glass walls and golden chandeliers, the kind of place where no one ever checks a price tag.

And there she is.

Diana — flawless in a deep bottle-red dress that fits like a secret, diamond earrings catching the light. Trouble, wrapped in elegance and a smile that knows it.

Keith is dropped off at a distance. He walks towards the entrance where Diana is waiting for him. She greets Keith with a kiss on the cheek, her perfume immediate and dangerous.

"You clean up well, Mr Keith. For a man who 'just happened' to bump into me." Diana's smile could melt glass.

"You invited me. I couldn't refuse destiny twice in one day." Keith replies with a slight grin.

She slips her arm into his, leading him inside.

The dining room is dim and intimate. Candles flicker in crystal holders. A soft jazz tune drifts from a corner stage where a pianist sways to his own rhythm. A waiter in a tux glides over as if on rails. Diana orders a bottle of red without looking at the menu — or at Keith.

"So, Keith…" She toys with the stem of her glass. "What is it you really do? You don't strike me as the 'aunt visiting' type."

"You caught me. I'm a professional conversationalist." Keith leans back, relaxed but alert.

"A liar, then." Her smile widens.

"Depends who's asking." His words come out smooth — too smooth. He meets her gaze, steady, but behind his calm exterior, he's dissecting every syllable, every flicker of her expression.

Beneath the table, his fingers tighten around the glass stem. He forces himself to breathe slowly — keep the rhythm, keep the mask.

The waiter glides in, silent as fog, setting down two plates — grilled sea bass with lemon butter for her, and a perfectly seared sirloin for him. The scent of rosemary and garlic fills the small space between them. Diana doesn't glance at her food; she's too busy watching him.

Outside, a black SUV sits half-hidden beneath a flickering streetlight. Inside, Ryan squints through binoculars — the wrong way around. "She's smiling," he mutters.

"That's either a good sign or she's about to rob him." He lowers the binoculars, grabs a croissant from the bakery bag, and takes a loud bite.

Melicia snatches the binoculars out of his hands. "Keep your eyes on her hands, not her lips."

"Easier said than done," Ryan mumbles, spraying crumbs and earning another glare.

On Melicia's lap, her tablet glows faintly — the feed from Keith's earpiece streaming in real time. She leans closer, jaw tight, as if sheer focus could protect him from whatever game Diana is playing inside.

Back in the restaurant, the wine's half gone. The air between them hums — light, smoky, dangerous. The candles throw soft, shifting gold across Diana's face, catching in her eyes like sparks.

"You mentioned your wife before..." she says, her tone silk with a hidden edge, stirring the sauce on her plate though she's barely eaten.

"Tragic. But tell me — do you believe in second chances?"

Keith sets down his knife and dabs the corner of his mouth with a napkin. "I believe in unfinished business."

Her eyes glint — part intrigue, part warning. "Then maybe we're both unfinished stories."

She lifted her hand slightly, signalling the waiter without breaking eye contact. Another bottle arrived — darker, heavier, the kind that stayed on your tongue long after the last sip. She poured for him first, her movements precise, her gaze steady.

"You strike me as a man who carries ghosts," she murmured. "Ones that don't let you sleep."

Keith took a slow sip, letting the wine burn before answering. "Maybe I just like keeping old memories company."

Her smile curved, soft but sharp. "That's dangerous. People who live in the past tend to miss what's right in front of them."

He met her eyes, calm but teasing, "And what's in front of me?"

Diana leaned in slightly, the candlelight dancing across her lips. "Me. For now."

Her fingers brushed his across the table — featherlight, calculated. Keith didn't pull away, though his pulse gave him away. The warmth of her touch was deceptive, like silk hiding a blade.

She was playing with him and testing him. And he knew it. But he played back anyway — the perfect act, smooth and steady. Because this wasn't a date, it was a negotiation masked as flirtation. A game neither could afford to lose.

Keith swirled his glass, keeping his tone casual. "You use that line often?"

Diana's smile deepened, lazy and knowing. "You always answer questions with more questions?"

He leaned back, lips tugging into a faint grin. "Only when I don't trust the person asking."

By now, dessert plates sat empty. The second bottle of wine lay half-drained, its scent thick in the air — like secrets neither of them was ready to spill.

Her gaze lingered on him — curious, assessing — before she lifted a hand for the waiter. "Check, please," she said smoothly, never breaking eye contact.

Then she rose, sliding her bag over one shoulder. "Come on," her voice dropped to a velvety command, silk wrapped around steel. "Let's get some air. I know a place you'll like."

His earpiece crackled. "Don't go," Melicia's voice snapped. "Keith, listen to me — something's off."

Keith hesitated, then whispered, "Relax," and switched off the mic.

Outside, the valet pulled up a sleek silver coupe, its surface glinting under the streetlights. Diana's heels struck the pavement in crisp rhythm as she approached.

They slid into the car — she in control, him pretending not to notice. What's with these women? Keith thought dryly as the engine purred to life. All of them are driving sports cars, while I'm out here feeling like a vintage sedan in a showroom full of Ferraris.

The city lights blurred behind them as Diana pushed the car faster. The night wind whipped through her hair, her perfume mixing with leather and tension. "So tell me, Keith…" she said, not looking at him. "Do you always follow women who lie to you?"

"Only when I think they're worth it."

Her laugh was soft — too soft. "Careful. Curiosity kills more than cats."

The car slowed. They rolled into a deserted stretch surrounded by empty fields.

Diana shifted in her seat, turning toward him. The dashboard light caught her eyes — glinting cold and silver. "Then let's make it interesting."

She leaned in, kissed him — deliberate, slow, almost real. Keith froze for a heartbeat, then played along. But something felt wrong. Her hands weren't exploring him — they were searching. Checking.

Miles behind, Ryan and Melicia watched through night-vision binoculars. "Well," Ryan said, chewing another croissant. "At least they're having a good time."

"This isn't the time for jokes," Melicia hissed. "Keith might be in danger."

"Nah," Ryan grinned. "He's having fun. Next time, send me. I'd kiss Diana better."

Melicia smacked his arm, eyes locked on the monitor.

Inside the car, Diana leaned in — close enough for Keith to catch the faint trace of her perfume. Her lips met his in a slow, deliberate kiss… then deepened, sudden and consuming, before she abruptly pulled away. It was like she'd lit a flame to prove she could extinguish it.

Keith let out a low, uneasy chuckle. "Disappointed?"

"Actually," she murmured, turning the key and bringing the engine back to life, "relieved. I want this evening to end… better."

He glanced at her, voice steady. "What do you have in mind?"

Her smile curved — soft, dangerous. "Patience, my love."

They drove in silence. The clock ticked past midnight. Diana's expression shifted — seductive no longer, but distant, calculating. She finally slowed near an apartment complex. Melicia's apartment.

Keith frowned. "Why here?"

Diana smiled thinly. "Because I like symmetry."

She pulled up across the street, the engine humming low. The silence between them stretched — fragile, final. Then she turned to him, voice soft but weighted now. "It was a wonderful evening, wouldn't you agree?"

Keith said nothing. His throat tightened; the act was over, and he knew it. She'd seen through every word.

Diana leaned closer, her perfume folding around him, her whisper brushing against his ear. "Goodbye, Keith."

He froze — and then came the dagger. "Tell Melicia that Van doesn't forgive mistakes. She has until eleven a.m. tomorrow to return the heirloom she stole."

Her lips lingered near his ear for a heartbeat longer. "I wish we'd met under different circumstances."

Before he could speak, she smiled — part sorrow, part warning — then turned the key. The car rolled away into the dark, taillights fading until they were nothing but two dying embers in the night.

Keith stood there in the glow of the streetlamp, realisation settling cold in his chest.
They'd been outplayed — beautifully, completely.

Melicia's car screeched to a stop behind him. She and Ryan jumped out, the smell of burnt rubber still hanging in the air. The three of them stood frozen, watching the red taillights vanish into the night.

They'd been played — every move, every word, a setup. Van and Diana hadn't just outsmarted them; they'd choreographed the entire evening to send a message.

From somewhere in the distance, the faint sound of Diana's laughter drifted through the wind — mocking, final.

For a long moment, no one spoke.

Melicia drew a sharp breath, pulled out her phone, and sent a single text — "We're on."

Seconds later, her screen flickered: "Okay."

They headed back to the apartment in silence.

"Well," Ryan finally muttered, tossing his jacket aside, "we tried."

Keith didn't reply. He just glanced at Melicia.

She met his gaze for a second before saying quietly, "You did well today. Honestly, I didn't think you'd get this far."

With that, she turned and walked toward the bedroom. At the doorway, she paused — gave him one brief, unreadable look — then disappeared inside.

Keith and Ryan sank into the couch, the weight of failure hanging between them.

"Man," Ryan sighed, rubbing his face, "these women… they play in a different league."

Keith stared at the floor, jaw tight. "Yeah," he said softly. "And we were just the warm-up act."

Later that night, Keith and Ryan were fast asleep, the faint hum of the air conditioner chilling the room to a crisp hush. Moonlight filtered through the half-drawn curtains, casting silver streaks across the rumpled sheets where the two men lay, their breathing deep and synchronised in the quiet rhythm of exhaustion.

The door creaked open with a slow, deliberate groan. Melicia stood there in the threshold, shadows tracing the soft curves of her face like forgotten secrets. Her eyes, dark and glistening with unspoken turmoil, found Keith in the dim light—peaceful, unaware, his chest rising and falling beneath the thin blanket. She stepped closer on bare feet, the cool floorboards whispering against her skin, and leaned over him. "Keith," she breathed, her voice a fragile thread in the night.

He stirred but didn't wake, his brow furrowing in sleep. She whispered again, softer this time, her voice trembling just enough to betray the storm of emotion churning beneath her calm exterior. His eyes blinked open, confused at first, lashes fluttering like moth wings—then widened in recognition when they locked onto hers.

"Come with me," she whispered, extending a hand that hovered in the air between them, an invitation laced with urgency.

Still half-asleep, Keith glanced back at Ryan, who was snoring loudly now, lost to the world in a tangle of limbs and dreams. Without a word, Keith slipped from the bed, his fingers brushing hers as he followed her down the hallway. The house felt alive with their footsteps—soft, conspiratorial—until Melicia led him into her room and closed the door behind them with a gentle click that sealed them in their own fragile bubble.

For a moment, silence reigned, thick and electric. The air between them was charged—part guilt for the lines they were crossing, part longing that had simmered unspoken for years, part something raw and buried they'd both tried to forget. The faint scent of her lavender shampoo mingled with the cool draft from the vent, wrapping around them like an invisible embrace.

"I couldn't sleep," she said softly, her gaze dropping to the floor before lifting to meet his. "Not after everything. Not after seeing you fight through it all to get here."

Keith looked at her, the distance between them shrinking with each heartbeat that echoed in his ears. He reached out, his thumb grazing the line of her jaw, feeling the warmth of her skin against the chill of the room. "You sure you want this?" he murmured, though even he didn't believe his own words; his voice was rough with the weight of restraint he was barely holding onto.

"Then stop me," she whispered, her breath warm against his lips as she closed the gap.

He didn't.

Melicia rose onto her toes, her hand brushing his cheek with a tenderness that made his heart stutter. He let out a quiet breath, surrendering as she leaned in. The kiss was slow—hesitant at first, a tentative exploration of lips that remembered each other all too well—then certain, deepening with the quiet certainty of inevitability. Her fingers threaded into his hair, pulling him closer, and for that fleeting moment, the world outside ceased to exist: no storms, no separations, no regrets—just the soft press of mouths and the shared ache of what had been lost and found.

She guided him gently toward the bed, their hands still intertwined, palms slick with the subtle tremor of anticipation. It wasn't rushed or wild, no frantic clawing at clothes or desperate grasps; it was something both had been holding back for far too long, a deliberate unravelling. They sank onto the mattress together, the sheets cool and inviting beneath them. Keith's hands traced the familiar lines of her back, pulling her against him as she straddled his lap, her forehead resting against his in the dim glow of the bedside lamp she'd flicked on low.

Melicia had left him once to protect him—from the dangers that shadowed her life, from the chaos she couldn't control. She'd walked away convinced it was the only way to keep him safe, even as it shattered something vital inside her.

And now, seeing him again—fighting through every storm, every obstacle, to reach her side—reminded her why she'd fallen for him in the first place. His quiet strength, the way he looked at her like she was both fragile and unbreakable, the unwavering loyalty that had pulled him back to her door.

Their movements were unhurried, intimate whispers of skin on skin as layers fell away. He kissed the hollow of her throat, tasting the salt of her tears mingled with desire; she arched into him, her nails grazing his shoulders in a plea for closeness. When they finally came together, it was with a sigh that spoke volumes—a reunion of bodies and souls, tender and profound. He moved inside her with a rhythm that mirrored the steady beat of their hearts, her name a reverent murmur on his lips. She clung to him, legs wrapped around his waist, feeling every inch of him as if reclaiming what was hers.

In the aftermath, they lay entwined, her head on his chest, listening to the thunder of his pulse slow to match hers. The air conditioner hummed on, oblivious. She didn't need him to survive—the world had taught her that much—but having him beside her, his fingers tracing lazy patterns on her spine, made the chaos almost bearable. In his arms, the storms felt distant, and for the first time, love felt like home.

By morning, Ryan woke up alone. He blinked at the space beside him, frowned, and dragged himself out of bed. As he stepped into the hallway, Melicia's door opened. Keith sat at the edge of her bed, hair a mess, face unreadable.

Ryan smirked. “Well, someone had a long night.”

Melicia ignored the jab, brushing past him to the kitchen. She poured herself a cup of coffee, movements calm, measured — almost too calm.

Ryan followed, voice sharper now. “We’ve got bigger problems, Mel. If that heirloom isn’t back by eleven, Van won’t just call — he’ll come for us.”

Keith emerged moments later, avoiding both their eyes. He went to the counter, and Melicia silently slid a mug toward him. Their fingers brushed — brief, deliberate — before he took it.

Ryan sighed. “So, I assume you’ve got a plan?”

Melicia’s lips curved into a faint, knowing smile. “Already in motion,” she said, her tone smooth and dangerous.

Chapter 14

This Wasn't In The Briefing

There was a knock at the door — heavy, deliberate. Ryan glanced at Melicia, then opened it.

Two of Van's men stood outside, dressed in black suits, faces unreadable.

"It's time," one of them said flatly.

Melicia didn't argue. She exchanged a quick look with Keith, then nodded.

They followed.

Outside, two black cars waited — engines running. Keith and Ryan were pushed into one; Melicia was led into the other. The convoy rolled off into the night, city lights fading into the distance. No one spoke.

After what felt like an hour, the cars turned through iron gates and up a long, winding drive. Van's mansion rose ahead — marble, glass, and arrogance.

Inside, the air smelled of expensive cigars and danger. Van lounged on a leather couch, Diana seated beside him, legs crossed, calm as ever.

Melicia stepped forward. "What's the meaning of this?" she demanded. "You still had until eleven. Why drag us here before the deadline?"

Van smiled — a predator's smile. "My dear Melicia. I think we both know you don't have the heirloom. Nor the ten million you promised me for stealing it in the first place."

"Here we go again," Melicia muttered under her breath.

Van rose slowly, his expression darkening, the charm slipping from his voice. "You underestimate me," he said, each word laced with warning.

Melicia didn't flinch. Her eyes lifted to meet his, steady and cold. "No, Van," she said quietly, "you underestimate me."

The words hung in the air like a drawn blade. Van stopped mid-stride, curiosity flickering behind his sharp gaze. "Where is it then?" he asked, his tone low, dangerous.

He moved toward her, measured steps echoing against the marble floor. Diana trailed close behind, her heels clicking softly — predatory. She shifted her attention to Keith, gliding closer until she stood beside him. Her manicured fingers brushed over his shoulder, tracing down his arm like a snake testing its prey. She leaned in, close enough for him to catch the scent of her perfume, and whispered, "Still as quiet as ever."

Keith didn't react. He met her gaze once, blank and unshaken, then turned away.

Van stopped inches from Melicia. She could feel his breath — warm, heavy with arrogance. "So?" he murmured. "Where's my heirloom?"

Melicia tilted her head slightly, her voice calm, almost casual. "You have Digger with you, don't you?"

Van frowned. "Why?"

"Get him," she said. "Now."

Van hesitated, searching her eyes for a clue, then motioned to his men. "Bring Digger." His smirk returned. "If this is a trick, Melicia, it won't end well for you. Buying time won't save you."

"You'll find out soon enough," she replied.

Moments later, two guards dragged Digger into the room. His face was bruised, his shirt torn, wrists bound. He looked like he'd been through hell.

Melicia's expression hardened. "Serves you right," she said icily. "You sold me out, and for once, Van did the right thing — throwing garbage where it belongs."

Van chuckled, clapping his hands once. "Now that we've reunited your little friend, maybe you'll finally tell me what this is all about."

But before Melicia could answer, the air shifted.

A faint wail echoed in the distance — faint at first, then growing louder.

SIRENS

Van's grin faltered. His men froze, exchanging alarmed glances. The sound drew closer, sharper — blue and red lights flashing through the tall glass windows.

"The hell—" Van began, spinning toward the door.

Then — **CRASH!**

The mansion doors burst open. Armed officers stormed in, shouting commands. "Police! Hands where we can see them!"

Chaos erupted — chairs overturned, glass shattered, and Van's men scrambled for cover.

The sirens died down outside the mansion, leaving a thick silence in their wake.

Melicia, Keith, and Ryan froze where they stood as the front doors burst open once more. Men in tactical black gear stormed in, weapons drawn, badges flashing.

"FBI!" one of them barked. "Nobody move!"

Van's expression twisted — half shock, half rage. "What the hell is the meaning of this?" he roared, his voice echoing through the grand hall. "Is this your doing, Melicia? You'll pay for this!"

"I have no idea what's going on!" Melicia shot back, her voice trembling slightly.

Keith and Ryan flinched, instinctively drawing close to each other. Van caught the movement — their startled reaction, their wide eyes — and for a brief moment, he knew. They weren't part of this. They had no clue the police were coming.

A tall officer stepped forward, his tone clipped and official. "We received a tip-off that stolen art was being hidden on these premises."

Van's eyes narrowed. "What stolen art?" he asked sharply.

The officer flipped open a folder, his tone calm but edged with authority. "Last night, a rare painting — The Scarlet Veil — was stolen from the National Museum." He laid out a printed sheet, the painting's image visible under the harsh basement light. "Satellite trace from the embedded tracker shows the signal originated right here." He tapped the map with a gloved finger. "We have a warrant to search the property."

Van's expression darkened, disbelief flashing into anger. He turned sharply toward his men, voice rising. "This is ridiculous!" he barked. "You think you can just walk in here with some baseless accusation?" He faced the officer again, eyes blazing. "My lawyers will bury this. I'll sue every last one of you for defamation before the day is over."

The officer didn't flinch. He closed the folder, eyes steady. "You can take it up with your lawyers, Mr Van. For now — step aside."

Before he could finish, another FBI agent approached Digger, who was still bound and bruised. The officer's brows lifted slightly. "Well, look who it is," he said with a dry chuckle. "Digger Miles. Art smuggler, forger, and a known associate of—" He glanced at Van. "—people who like to keep expensive hobbies."

Digger swallowed, saying nothing.

"So," the officer continued, circling him slowly. "The entire crew's here. The mastermind, the muscle, and…" his gaze flicked to Van, "…the money man."

Van's jaw tightened. "He's not with me," he snapped. "He's with them."

The agent's gaze shifted to Melicia, Keith, and Ryan. "Oh? So, this is your team, then?"

Melicia exhaled quietly, steadying her voice. "We're just visiting Van. We were about to leave."

"No one leaves this room," the officer said coldly. He motioned to his men. "Search everything."

Footsteps echoed through the marble corridors, sharp and deliberate. The search teams spread out like shadows, their radios crackling faintly in the background. Drawers were yanked open, papers scattered like snow. A chair crashed to the floor, followed by the low thud of boots moving closer, closer.

Then — clang! — a metallic sound reverberated from somewhere deep beneath the mansion, hollow and cold, like a secret the walls themselves were forced to reveal.

Diana slowly pulled out her phone, her fingers trembling slightly as she searched online — art robbery news… is this even real? Within seconds, the headline on the "Daily News" appeared on her screen.

"The Scarlet Veil Stolen from the National Museum."

Her eyes widened. She lifted her gaze toward Van. He caught the reflection of the headline on her phone's screen before meeting her stare again. His stomach dropped. This was real. Genuine.

But why the hell would they think I have it? Van thought, a cold wave crawling down his spine.

"Sir!" one of the agents called out. "We found something."

Everyone turned. The agent stood near the grand fireplace, where the floor panel had been pried open — revealing a narrow staircase leading underground.

The lead officer's lips curled into a grim smile. "Well, Mr Van. Care to lead the way?"

Van's face drained of colour. "That's… private property."

The officer raised a brow. "So is theft. Open it."

After a long pause, Van descended first, with the officers close behind. The underground passage reeked of age — the scent of old stone, damp air, and lingering moisture filled the narrow space. It felt ancient, as though this place had existed for decades, perhaps centuries. The mansion had belonged to Van's family for generations, its walls concealing hidden passages, secret pathways, and unknown entrances. No one knew where this one led — until they reached the end, where a massive steel vault loomed in the darkness.

"Open it," the officer ordered again, his voice echoing off the cold stone walls.

Van hesitated, his hand hovering over the keypad. One of the officers stepped forward, his tone sharp and uncompromising. "If you don't open it, we'll force it. And we're not responsible for any damage that happens in the process."

Van had always managed to get his way — smooth talk, powerful connections, and an army of lawyers ready to clean up his messes. But he wasn't foolish. This time, resistance would only make things worse. For now, it was better to cooperate, to let the storm pass and let his legal team handle the rest later.

He swallowed his pride, masking his arrogance beneath a calm façade, and entered the code. A heavy metallic click echoed through the chamber, followed by a long, low groan as the steel door began to shift. Dust drifted down from the ceiling as the vault creaked open, releasing a breath of stale, warm air tinged with the scent of metal and age.

Light flickered into the room. The officers' flashlights swept across the interior — stacks of tightly bound cash rising like miniature towers, rows of velvet boxes glittering with jewels, and bundles of brittle, yellowed documents stamped with old family crests. The vault glimmered like a forgotten kingdom preserved beneath the earth.

And there, at the very centre, encased within a glass pedestal, rested a single ornate heirloom — a masterpiece of gold filigree set with rubies and emeralds, radiating a quiet, undeniable allure. The officers exchanged glances. There was no doubt about it.

It was the same artefact that was stolen from the National Museum ten years ago.

The officers exchanged sharp glances. One, barely concealing a smirk, muttered under his breath, “Well, well. Looks like we just cracked a cold case.” The words sent an electric current through the room.

Van spun toward them, breath shallow, eyes wild. “That— that’s mine! It was stolen from my family years ago, I—”

“Save it,” the agent snapped, cutting him off. “You can explain it downtown.”

Hands moved with professional precision. Within minutes, Van, Diana, and Van’s men were cuffed — the metallic click sealing the moment with a cold finality that echoed against the vault’s walls. Melicia, Keith, and Ryan, who lingered by the threshold, were quickly restrained as well, “for further questioning,” one officer stated, tone clipped and unyielding.

The quiet grandeur of the mansion dissolved into the harsh rhythm of law enforcement — the hiss of leather straps, the sharp clicks of zip ties, the rustle of uniforms.

Outside, the sun hung high above the estate. Red and blue lights strobed across the gravel driveway, flashing against the hedges and polished car doors in alternating waves.

Van was shoved toward a waiting police van, shoulders jolted, boots grinding against the stone path. The metal door loomed before him, its cold scent of steel and rain filling his lungs. Before they could push him in, he leaned close to one of the FBI agents, voice low and venomous.

“You and I both know this is nonsense,” he hissed. “I’ll be out before you even reach the station.”

The agent didn't flinch, didn't even look at him. Van's tone shifted, softening into something more dangerous. "I can make this… disappear. Five million. Cash."

The agent's eyes flicked up, amused. "Five? That's cute." His lips curled into a smirk. "Ten — and maybe your record gets 'misplaced.'"

Van's glare burned for a long second before he exhaled sharply. "Fine. Ten."

Back inside, Diana's men moved like shadows, slipping into the mansion and returning with black duffel bags bulging with cash. The officer unzipped one and began counting, bills snapping under his gloved fingers with ritual precision. He nodded once, subtle and deliberate, before signalling his team.

"Van, Diana, and the gentlemen — you're free to go. The confiscated heirloom and other jewellery will be reviewed and verified at the station. If they're found to be legitimately yours, they'll be returned," the officer announced, his tone smooth and strictly professional.

Relief and restrained fury flickered across Van's face as the cuffs came off. He flexed his wrists, rubbing the red marks left by the steel. Outside, the flashing lights washed over him in alternating waves of crimson and blue, casting shifting shadows across his expression — half triumph, half contempt.

The officer's gaze shifted to Melicia and her team. His tone cooled. "… The others stay put."

Van adjusted his suit, straightening the lapel with deliberate calm. As he strode past Melicia, he paused, letting a slow smirk curl across his face. "You play dirty, Mel," he murmured, voice dripping with arrogance. "But I play deeper. The heirloom — I'll get it back. I always do."

Melicia glared at him, her eyes sharp with betrayal. "You made a fool of me," she said quietly. "You had the heirloom all along."

Van tilted his head slightly, his smirk never fading. "A price you pay," he said, voice low and cutting, "for stealing from me."

Melicia's jaw tightened, but she said nothing more. Keith gently placed a hand on her shoulder, guiding her back as Van walked away — his figure disappearing into the strobing lights and the sound of engines fading into the distance.

The convoy rolled away from the mansion, engines humming under the night sky.

For several miles, no one spoke. Then, suddenly, the lead police van pulled off the main road and into a deserted clearing.

The engine shut off. Silence.

Keith frowned. "What's going on?"

One of the "FBI agents" turned from the front seat — and grinned. "What's going on?" he repeated. "We're clocking out."

Then, to everyone's shock, the men began peeling off their vests, unzipping jackets, pulling off fake badges. The letters "FBI" came away like stickers. Underneath — plain clothes.

Melicia exhaled, a grin breaking through her calm facade. "Finally."

Ryan blinked. "Wait—what—"

The "officer" nearest her removed his cap and laughed. "You still love your theatrics, don't you, Mel?"

Keith looked between them, confused. "Who the hell is this?"

Melicia smiled. "Keith, Ryan… meet Leo. Old friend. Former partner in crime."

Leo gave a mock bow. "Long time, Mel. You still know how to pull off a heist with style."

Ryan's jaw dropped. "You planned this?"

Melicia leaned back, stretching her arms. "Of course. Van thought he could play me. I just gave him a show he'd never forget."

Keith shook his head, half impressed, half exasperated. "You're insane."

"Maybe," Melicia said, her grin widening, "but it worked."

Leo tossed Melicia a set of car keys, the metal glinting under the dim streetlight.

"Your ride's waiting a few blocks ahead," he said with a smirk. "Oh, and the heirloom?" He gave a wink. "It'll be couriered straight to the museum."

Melicia chuckled, exhaustion mixing with relief. "That works. The last thing we need is Van tracking us again. He'll probably try to steal it back once he realises he's been played. But for now…" She exhaled, satisfied. "That should keep him off our backs."

Leo grinned, tugging off his fake badge and tossing it into the van. Van paid ten million to fake cops. Not bad for a night's work, huh?"

Everyone burst out laughing — Melicia's laughter leading the chorus, loud and free for the first time in days. Keith and Ryan, however, just stared — still trying to process what happened.

"So… all this was a setup?" Keith finally asked, rubbing his temples. "The raid, the police, even the shouting?"

Melicia tilted her head, pretending to think. "Hmm, yep. Pretty much everything except your shocked face. That was genuine."

Ryan crossed his arms, still sulking. "You could've told us, y'know. Maybe spared me from a mild heart attack?"

She smirked. "And miss that priceless reaction? Not a chance."

Ryan groaned dramatically. "Next time, try laughing at someone else's expense. My blood pressure can't take another fake arrest."

Leo laughed, clapping Ryan's shoulder. "Kid, you've got potential. But you panic too soon." He then handed Melicia a small black duffel bag. "For your troubles," he said.

Melicia raised an eyebrow. "Generous as always."

Leo's crew started their engines, peeling off into the night.

Melicia, Keith, and Ryan walked down the quiet block toward a waiting car. The afternoon sun bathed the street in a gentle warmth, glinting off the windows and casting long, lazy shadows along the empty footpath — a scene they never thought they'd see again. Each step felt lighter, the air cleaner, the silence almost soothing. After everything, it was good to be out of danger. Relief washed over them in waves — the simple essence of freedom, sharp and sweet, tasted better than they'd ever remembered.

They eased into the car; the engine purred to life, and the faint rattle of cooling metal filled the quiet.

Keith turned in his seat, eyes fixed on Melicia. "Alright, Mel. Spill it. How long have you been planning this?"

Melicia drummed her fingers once on the steering wheel, a slow grin curving her lips. "Since the night we realised the heirloom was never with Dr Stevins," she said, voice calm but edged with satisfaction. The indicator ticked softly as she turned onto the empty street. "I knew Van had set Diana up as bait — classic move. He stirs chaos, watches who crawls out, then strikes. His men had been shadowing us from the very beginning."

Ryan leaned forward from the back seat, curiosity burning through his exhaustion. "So that's why you locked yourself in your room — not exactly beauty sleep, you were planning, huh?"

Melicia's eyes glinted in the rearview mirror. "Exactly. I needed them to think I was cracking under pressure — emotional, unstable — while Leo and his team staged the fake FBI raid: uniforms, fake badges, staged vehicles, even a fake warrant. Van's arrogance did the rest. He thought he was untouchable." She rolled her shoulders back, exhaling as if releasing hours of hidden tension.

Ryan raised a brow. "Okay, but explain this — how did you pull off the whole Scarlet Veil stunt? The news said it was stolen from the National Museum."

Melicia chuckled, the corners of her mouth curling into a smirk. "It wasn't stolen," she said. "It was faked — made to look stolen."

Keith frowned. "But the news report— it showed the heist, security footage, everything."

"All recycled," Melicia said, eyes still on the road. "We took the real report from a couple of years ago, changed the dates, reuploaded it through a ghost server, and made sure it trended just long enough for Van's men to believe it was fresh."

Keith sat back, half-amazed, half-exasperated. "You could've told us, Mel. We could've helped."

Melicia gave a soft, apologetic smile. "I couldn't risk it. Van's reach is long, and if he caught wind of what I was doing, it would've been you two paying the price. This was my mess to clean up — my score to settle. Van's been tormenting me for years. Tonight, he finally tripped over his own shadow."

Ryan let out a low whistle, leaning back with his arms behind his head. "You sure know how to end things dramatically — fake sirens, fake arrests, ten million dollars on the table. What's next? A Netflix deal?"

Melicia rolled her eyes, a reluctant grin tugging at her lips. "Keep talking, Ryan, and I'll make you the next decoy."

Keith chuckled, shaking his head as the tension in the car finally eased into quiet relief. "You two are impossible," he said, but his voice carried a note of admiration.

As the car sped away, laughter filled the cabin, blending with the hum of the engine — the sound of victory, quiet and fleeting, before the world caught up again.

Ryan pointed to the black duffel bag sitting at Melicia's feet. "Alright, serious question — what's in the bag? Please tell me it's not another 'surprise.'"

Melicia smirked, one hand on the wheel. "You could say it's our... pay check."

Ryan's eyes widened. "Pay check? As in a money paycheck?"

"Leo's cut from Van's donation to the 'fake FBI foundation,'" she said with a wink.

Ryan nearly jumped from his seat. "Oh, hallelujah! We actually get paid for nearly dying?!"

Melicia burst out laughing. "Don't get too excited."

"So how much is my share?" Ryan asked, grinning ear to ear.

Melicia glanced at him through the rearview mirror. "Remember that sports car you've been dreaming about?"

Ryan froze. "Don't mess with me, Mel."

She smiled. "Well… your dreams just came true, Ryan."

He gasped theatrically, clapping his hands. "You mean—wait, I can finally buy the car? The red one with the spoiler?!"

Keith sighed. "And that's the only thing you took from tonight."

Ryan grinned proudly. "Everyone's got priorities, man. You have trauma; I have turbo."

Melicia shook her head, laughing as they turned onto the highway. "You're ridiculous."

"Ridiculously loyal," Ryan said, winking. "And rich now, apparently."

Keith chuckled, leaning back as the city lights came into view. "We should really get normal jobs."

Melicia smirked. "For once, I agree on that."

The car sped down the empty road, headlights cutting through the dark. Three shadows against the glow — one cunning, one grounded, one chaotic.

And somewhere behind them, in a mansion full of confusion and missing millions, Van seethed — already plotting his next move.

A year later, Melicia's phone buzzed on the table.

Unknown Message:

You up for a job?

Leo.

She stared at it for a long second, then sighed. Without replying, she set the phone down, the screen dimming like a secret left untouched.

Keith was on the couch, half-buried in cushions, shouting at the football match like the players could actually hear him. Melicia slipped beside him, curling her legs up and leaning into his side. Without a word, she took his hand.

For a while, the only sounds were the roar of the crowd and Keith's occasional frustrated groan. Then, quietly, she leaned in and kissed his cheek — soft, deliberate. Her fingers brushed through his hair.

"I'm bored," she murmured. "This life— too quiet. I want action."

Keith blinked, then turned to her, eyes wide. "You too?" he said, almost relieved. "If I have to spend one more week cataloguing German poetry and arguing with retirees about overdue books, I might lose my mind."

Melicia laughed, the sound light and wicked. "So, the librarian wants danger now?"

He grinned back. "Librarian-slash-German-translator, thank you very much. And yes— I was hoping you'd say that. What took you so long?"

She tilted her head, eyes glinting. "I was waiting to see if you'd crack first."

He feigned offence, clutching his heart. "You used me as a boredom experiment?"

"Maybe," she teased, brushing his hair again. "But you passed."

Outside, the night murmured with a quiet rhythm; inside, the two of them sat shoulder to shoulder, wrapped in the kind of silence that felt like peace— and promise.

• • •

Author's Note

This book began with the intention of being a serious love story — Melicia and Keith were originally meant to be wrapped in drama, tension, and heavy emotions. But somewhere during the writing process, I realised that the world already has plenty of intense romances, and I didn't want this one to blend into the crowd. I wanted something different. I wanted a romance that didn't rely on long speeches, a connection that didn't need melodrama, and a story that wasn't afraid to mix danger with humour, messiness with sincerity, and chaos with heart.

That's when Ryan appeared — unplanned, ridiculous, and absolutely perfect. His presence shifted everything. What was once a dark, suspenseful plot became a more cinematic ride: thrilling, funny, emotional, and wonderfully unpredictable.

Melicia became the storm with a secretive, complicated past; Keith became the quiet spark she didn't know she needed; and Ryan became the lovable disaster stuck between them. Keith was never meant to be her first love, but he became the one that mattered — a simple man whose steady heart grounded her wildness. And Keith himself represents many of us: people living simple, peaceful lives who secretly wonder what it would feel like to be thrown into an adventure. Ryan, the friend everyone wishes they had, stayed by Keith's side through every insane moment because that's what loyal idiots do.

In the end, Melicia led them both through danger, madness, and moments they never thought they could survive. What started as a serious story transformed into a journey of unexpected love, foolish bravery, and reckless loyalty.

I truly hope readers enjoy the thrill, warmth, comedy, and unpredictability as much as I loved writing A Lady, A Kiss and Two Idiots.

Available On Most Online Stores

9 789355 257901

Printed at Repro India Ltd.